The *Home Front*

GUIDE TO DOING UP YOUR PERIOD HOME

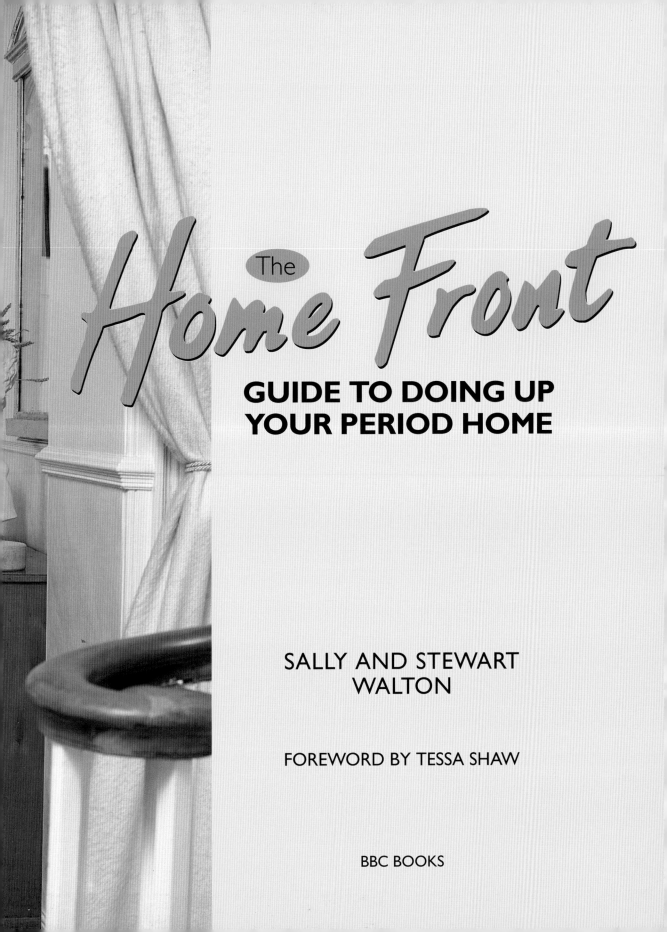

The Home Front

GUIDE TO DOING UP
YOUR PERIOD HOME

SALLY AND STEWART
WALTON

FOREWORD BY TESSA SHAW

BBC BOOKS

This book is published to accompany the fourth
BBC Television series of **Home Front**, broadcast in 1997
Editor Daisy Goodwin

Published by BBC Books,
an imprint of BBC Worldwide Publishing.
BBC Worldwide Limited, Woodlands,
80 Wood Lane, London W12 0TT

First published 1997
© Sally and Stewart Walton 1997
The moral right of the authors has been asserted

ISBN 0 563 37161 7

Designed by DW Design
Illustrations © Kevin Hart 1997
Picture research by Vivian Adelman

Printed in Great Britain by Cambus Litho Ltd, East Kilbride
Bound in Great Britain by Hunter & Foulis Ltd, Edinburgh
Colour separations by Radstock Reproductions Ltd, Midsomer Norton
Jacket printed by Lawrence Allen Ltd, Weston-super-Mare

PREVIOUS SPREAD *An entrance hall of an early Victorian house with a wealth of original features. The warmth of polished wood, old flagstones and creamy white walls and drapes contrasts with the dramatic pattern of the rag rug. Nothing has been taken away from this period house but new life has been added, making it all the richer.*

OPPOSITE *A charming plaster detail on a modest Victorian terraced house.*

contents

foreword

In the 1960s it was fashionable to 'modernize' period houses, and skirting boards, cornices, old fireplaces and baths were often ruthlessly ripped out. Now new owners are much more likely to be feverishly trying to put them back. Architectural salvage yards have never been busier.

Because of this, the BBC's *Home Front* team decided to run a weekly feature on restoring a period home, and we found the Walsh family, Graham and Maxine and their children Vicky and Luis, who wanted to do up their newly acquired house themselves. The Walshes were lucky that their house, in Pudsey on the outskirts of Leeds, had never been properly modernized and still had many of its original features, but they also spent long hours searching out specialist suppliers to help them re-create missing or damaged features. Viewers shared in the experience of discovering and renovating a huge blackened kitchen range; of designing a new panel of stained glass for their reclaimed front door; of moving the magnificent porcelain tub to pride of place in the bathroom; and of decorating

THE HOME FRONT GUIDE

BELOW *Graham and Maxine Walsh. Watching them tackle the restoration of their late Victorian house on Home Front became compulsive viewing.*

their sitting room in an ornate period style. The response from the audience was immediate and enthusiastic, and each episode brought a deluge of requests for Fact Sheets and sacks of mail from viewers wanting more information. The need for an accessible general guide to restoring and renovating period houses became clear – and *The Home Front guide to doing up your period home* was born.

The book shows you what the Walshes – who had no previous experience and a limited budget – achieved with a little expert advice from *Home Front.* We hope that wherever you live and whatever your budget, it will give you the encouragement and the confidence to have a go.

introduction

Renovating a period home is like embarking on a fascinating, often thrilling, voyage of discovery. Your eyes will be opened, perhaps for the first time, to the richness of detailing, both inside and out, that characterize 'your' period. You will almost certainly develop a passionate appreciation of the original features that still remain and an equally fervent envy of many that you observe in the houses of friends. When you come to do up your house, you will – like the Walshes – want to preserve, restore or reinstate those features that give your home its authentic period flavour. At the same time you will probably wish to enjoy those creature comforts that are taken for granted in modern living. *The Home Front guide to doing up your period home* shows how to plan and achieve a restoration that skilfully incorporates the technical advances of the second half of the twentieth century within a period setting.

This is not a specialist technical manual, nor an in-depth treatment of period detail for the purist. It is a practical guide to the procedures and processes of renovation. It will help you make informed decisions from the start – alerting you to the need for planning permission as well as to the possibilities of financial help, in the form of grants, for your restoration. It will help you assess which jobs you can manage yourself and which are probably best left to the experts. An important section of the book explains how to get the best out of the people you employ, such as architects and builders, while getting exactly what you want. Names of specialist suppliers and services are given throughout the book, and their addresses, together with supplementary useful addresses, are listed at the end of the book on pages 186–189.

In some cases it may not be a practical option to restore the inside of your house to its original style. It is important, however, that any original external features are preserved, restored or replicated. In a Conservation Area you are bound by law, as you are with a listed building, to preserve the character of your home. If your home does not fall into these categories, find out if your local authority has set up a Conservation Department, with officers responsible for advising owners of period homes on sympathetic, appropriate ways of handling repairs.

No matter how simple or how grandiose your plans for restoration, always take your time. Consider all the implications, both short- and long-term, of the changes you are going to make to the house and do not be tempted by quick-fix solutions. If, for example, you have a problem with damp in the cellar, careful unblocking of ventilation ducts and a gradual drying out and airing process is more likely to offer a satisfactory long-term solution than a quick injection of chemical damp-proofing.

Those readers who also saw the *Home Front* weekly features with the Walshes will relate at once to the sections (at the end of many of the chapters) based on their personal experiences. Most people are far more likely to be inspired to cook an exotic dish if they have seen their favourite television chef show how it's done, rather than simply read it in a recipe book. And in the same way that most of us would rather read agony columns than weighty tomes on psychology, the renovation process is rendered far less daunting for those who watched the

BELOW *Period features don't have to be removed to create a contemporary look. This room has original radiators, skirtings, cornices, floorboards and a fabulous fireplace. The colours and finishes bring it up to date leaving the choice of a more traditional restoration open for future occupants.*

Home Front series simply because they have seen it in action. Designing your own front door, complete with stained-glass panel and traditional fittings, becomes a real possibility when you have seen Maxine and Graham working on it step-by-step, from the moment of the original purchase of a second-hand door in a reclamation yard. The Walshes had no previous experience of owning or restoring an old house. The message is clear: if they can do it, so can you.

a voyage of discovery

your house has a past of which you are destined to become a part, because it also has a future. The two are inseparably linked and finding out about your house's past can become a fascinating sideline to your restoration job. Your discoveries may well influence the decisions that you make about the style of your restoration.

If your house is very old it is likely to be a listed building whose history has already been documented, but all period houses have a story to tell and even the humblest of former residents' lives take on a certain fascination when you are living within the same walls as they once did. The house itself may not immediately offer you many clues, but they will be there for you once you turn house detective.

The first place to look is up and down the street. If yours is a Georgian, Victorian or Edwardian town house, it is unlikely to be the only one of its kind and there may even be elderly residents who have lived in similar neighbouring houses for most of their lives. Such people are often very willing to talk about the past, so, having explained your interest, prompt their memories to find out about the changes that they have seen over the years and the people who lived in your house before you. They may be happy to let you have a look around their homes as well. Then, since houses only usually undergo major changes when they pass into new hands, you may find yourself stepping right back in time.

The estate agent, surveyor and your solicitor can often be helpful if you make them aware of your interest in the house's history. If the agents are a long-established local firm, they may have old records themselves or they may recall previous owners who investigated the house's history. In the excitement and tension of the buying process it is easy to forget to ask whether the people you are buying from know anything about the house or its previous occupants, but they have probably left a forwarding address, and a tentative enquiry could prove rewarding. Tread carefully though, because people leave houses for many reasons and not all are happy ones.

Surveyors have to look into all nooks and crannies, checking the cellar, loft and staircase, as well as examining the floorboards, plasterwork, windows and doors. All these could yield valuable clues, but you need to make the surveyor aware of your interest in advance because the standard report is about the soundness of the structure and is unlikely to include romantic discoveries such as lovers' initials and a date carved under the staircase.

Your solicitor will have had a 'search' conducted on your behalf, to discover whether any ancient rights of way or other claims to your land exist, and may in the process have come across interesting documents relating to previous owners' occupations and activities, or even those of their immediate neighbours. He may also have held on to old deeds relating to your property, or will at least be able to advise you of their likely whereabouts. The mortgage company holds the deeds that relate directly to your purchase of the house, and will send photocopies for a small fee. Go through these carefully in search of clues.

A trip to the reference section of your local library should prove fruitful. There they house copies of all Ordnance Survey maps of the area, local history books and photographic records, plus street directories, the equivalent

of the modern telephone book, giving the names and professions or trades of house occupants, arranged alphabetically, street by street. These were published locally annually, but not in all areas of the country. You should be able to take photocopies of the entries that relate to your house. Keep a file with all these snippets of information that help to build up a picture of the house's past life.

The library will also have a list of any local groups that may be able to help you. These include local history groups, architectural conservation groups, geological and archaeological societies. A conservation group often consists of owners of historic houses, architects and campaigners, who appreciate the value of preserving old buildings in the area. They may have records relating to your house, especially if it was part of a larger development by a local builder, or if it has figured in any redevelopment plans that have been fought and blocked. Such groups will always welcome enquiries from people who intend to preserve the character and integrity of an old building.

Local historians will be able to tell you about changes that have taken place in your area and about the sort of people – ordinary, famous or notorious – who lived there in the past. Archaeological societies can enlighten you on the distant past and any important discoveries that have been unearthed, as well as inspect any 'finds' you may make when digging your new garden. Local amateur geologists can analyse bricks to discover the origin of their clay and will also help identify local stone or flint that has been used in your house.

Other possible sources of information include the local government archives, housed in the County Record Office, the local museum,

local newspapers and the parish register of the local church. There are also national societies that can be extremely helpful and their names and addresses are listed on page 186. They include The Society for the Protection of Ancient Buildings (SPAB), The Georgian Group, The Victorian Society and English Heritage. Each one has a specific area of interest and will often be able to pass your enquiry on to somebody whom you can contact locally.

There are some very good books that deal solely with discovering a house's history and they are listed on page 189. If you suspect that your house has an interesting story to tell, one or two of these books are well worth reading.

Clues to house dating

Early houses were always built from locally available materials, so where there was a good supply of stone, flint, clay, lime or hardwood,

LEFT *A terrace of typically flat-fronted late Georgian town houses, with elegant wrought-iron details, and stucco on the lower two storeys and the cornice. Printed pattern and plan books made it possible for similar styles to be copied by builders in all parts of the country: previously architectural styles had been very localized. Conformity to the prevailing notions of classical proportion became the rule.*

CENTRE *A mid-Victorian terrace in a country town, built in the Gothic Revival manner. This style encouraged individual houses within a terrace to become more varied, with distinctive details such as* *the carved wooden fretwork and bargeboarding on the gables. The arched windows here are casements but sashes were also made in this style.*

RIGHT *A mass-produced late Victorian terrace with recessed porchways, plenty of decorative plasterwork and projecting bay windows which give a good view of the street and let in the maximum light. Builders worked from standard plans and chose decorative details from large catalogues according to their own preferences, which is why the same features appear in different combinations throughout the country.*

builders made use of it. Only the very wealthy could afford to transport building materials over long distances before the rail network was developed in the middle of the nineteenth century.

Bricks

Bricks were used by the Romans but subsequently fell from use until reintroduced on a large scale in Tudor times. There was a reaction against timber-framed buildings after the Great Fire of London in 1666 and brick production all over the country soared. Most towns had their own brickworks and used local clay. Clay colours vary a lot and bricks can be analysed to discover their origin. A brick tax was in force between 1784 and 1850, which prompted the use of the rendered plaster known as stucco and alternative types of cladding, such as tiling and weatherboarding. Bricks were laid in different ways, called bonds, at different periods and can be helpful in establishing the date of a building.

Windows

Glass was not used in windows before the sixteenth century and windows were small, to prevent intrusion. Early glass could only be made in small pieces and these were held together in a frame of lead strips that were fixed into the walls. Windows that could be opened were originally hinged; sash windows became common towards the end of the seventeenth century. The Georgian sashes had smaller panes than the Victorian ones, because the method of making large sheets of window glass only developed after the 1830s. A window tax existed between 1695 and 1851, which is why you often see bricked-up windows in old houses. The tax was eventually abolished when the Public Health Act of 1848 was introduced

to bring people's standard of living up to a healthier level by making the installation of adequate drainage, sanitation and ventilation enforceable by law.

Building styles

Early houses were built by local craftsmen using traditional local materials and methods, and it was not until Renaissance ideas were imported from Europe by the nobility in the sixteenth century that anything like a fashionable national style developed. The development of iron printing presses in the late eighteenth century enabled books of architectural plans to be published and circulated to builders around the country.

The Georgian period (roughly 1700–1800) was distinguished mainly by the strikingly elegant proportions and simplicity of its buildings. Town houses were characterized by parapets that concealed the roof line from the street, a symmetrical arrangement of windows, and a front door, often framed by classical-style pillars, with a semi-circular fanlight above it to let the light into the entrance hall.

The Regency period (roughly 1800–1825) produced houses that were essentially more delicate, more ornamental variations of the Georgian style. Regency style was especially popular in seaside towns like Brighton and Hastings, where fine examples still abound. Houses often had bow fronts, first-floor balconies with elegant awnings and fine wrought-ironwork railings.

The Victorian period (roughly 1825–1900) saw many changes. Early Victorian buildings were much influenced by Italian architecture and feature rounded arched windows, stucco columns and shallow pitched roofs. Later, a reaction against the 'pagan' classically influenced style of Georgian architecture led to the Gothic

Revival. Houses were built to resemble small churches, with high pitched roofs, arched windows and stained-glass panels that imitated the much admired cathedral architecture of the Middle Ages. The style filtered through all types of building work. There was a massive expansion of towns and cities at this time because of increasing industrialization and the need for workers' houses. Whole suburbs were built by speculative builders and similar plans were used all over the country. Although the houses were mass-produced, they were generally well built and even the humblest had features that we now find 'desirable', such as cast-iron and slate fireplaces, solidly constructed wooden staircases and sash windows.

The Edwardian period (roughly 1900–1915) produced houses that are often very similar to those built in the late Victorian period. There is often a mixing of styles –Tudor-style timbered upper storeys over recessed fretwork porches with pebble-dashed walls, for example. Semi-detached houses became more popular than terraced houses, each with a strip of garden, not just a yard. Influences from the Arts and Crafts movement and Art Nouveau are apparent in details such as stylized floral motifs and curvilinear patterns in stained glass, while the Queen Anne Revival brought Dutch-style gables and the liberal use of terracotta tiles and fancy brick courses. Houses were still being built, streets at a time, to standard plans and any variations usually stemmed from the builder's own preferences. If your house is of this period you should not have any trouble in discovering its basic history, as full records were being kept by this time.

Interpreting clues

The dating of a house by examining individual pieces, such as a section of timber, tiling or decorative iron- or plasterwork, can be misleading because the idea of recycling building materials is not a new one. When these materials had to be quarried or cut by hand, it made sense to re-use stone and timbers wherever possible. This practice continued and was especially prevalent in country house building where you may discover that the roof beams pre-date the house by a hundred years. If you come across a feature that strikes you as unusual, it is always worth investigating its origin, to discover whether it has been there since the beginning or is a whimsical later addition.

Inside the house, the style of the staircase, fireplace, flooring, plasterwork, skirting boards, doors and architraves are reliable dating clues if they match up to the external features, especially if other houses in your street share the same style. On a small scale, the window fittings and door furniture of a Georgian, Victorian or Edwardian house are unlikely to have been replaced in the style of the period unless it was done quite recently, when the reproduction market really took off. So, if these features seem to be original, examine them for a maker's name, which could date them very accurately. One final clue that is worth noting is that the penny post was only introduced in 1840 and front doors dating before that time had no letterboxes (although many subsequently had them put in). The postal system made it important for houses to have consecutive numbers as well, and these are another original feature that may still exist on your house, in the form of an engraved brass plate or individual brass numerals.

In a similar way to probing family history, this kind of detective work has the special quality of being a very personal pursuit; and whether your quest is of passing or obsessive interest, it cannot fail to fascinate.

THE WALSHES' HOUSE HISTORY

street plans were lodged with the local council. There they found that their house had been built within six months of a local almshouse, which was firmly dated to 1895. They also learned that the builder had sold the house to a Harold Parker. To discover more, they looked at the electoral registers. The earliest one in the library was dated 1936 and the occupants were still the Parker family. Harold Parker was a town hall employee and an electrical engineer, responsible for the street lighting of Pudsey. He lived in the house with his wife Sarah and their son Harold Jnr. The relatively high status of Mr Parker's job would account for certain quality features in the house, such as the kitchen range and the mahogany newel post and hand rail of the staircase.

In order to find out more, the Walshes arranged for local historian Daru Rooke to pay them a visit at the house. As he said, 'One of

The same woman had lived in the Crawshaw Street house for fifty years before the Walsh family took it over and although it had been well kept, redecoration had been minimal. The fireplaces, staircase and bathroom suite were all original and a fantastic kitchen range was discovered hidden behind a sheet of board in the chimney breast. Graham and Maxine were interested to find out as much as possible about the house's history, and the lifestyle of its previous occupants.

Their first stop was the Leeds Reference Library, where they went through the Ordnance Survey maps to find out when the house was built. The 1892 map showed Crawshaw Street as Field Number 99, but the 1908 map showed that the house had already been built. The Walshes discovered that descendants of the original builder still lived in the street, and through them learned that the

the give-away points that the house is nearer 1900 than 1870 is the stained glass. Although the type of stained glass had been on the go for thirty years, the colours here are paler and more subdued – and these started to come in towards the turn of the century.'

He was also able to tell them that the fireplaces in their house dated from the later 1890s and that the one in the front room, or parlour, was made of slate, which would have been grained to imitate marble. He dated the range to a similar time, noting that it was larger and more ornate than was usual for such a tiny kitchen. He described the daily life of the maid who would have had to clean and cook for the family and was interested to hear that Graham had found a hot-water pipe leading outside from the range. This showed that there would have been outhouses (now demolished), including a washroom and water closet. The cellar, even though it was empty, had not changed at all. The large stone slab shelf would have served as the cold store for perishable food as the kitchen would have been very hot because of the range. There was also a coal bunker with a shute leading down from the back of the house.

The bathroom was a mixture of different periods, with a 1930s glass splashback behind the original basin. The bath was boxed in during the 1950s, and the loo replaced at about the same time.

Gaslight was considered to be unhealthy in bedrooms, but the attic room, where the maid would have slept, did have gas fittings. Being first up and last to bed, mostly in the hours of darkness, she would have needed the lights. The attic room had only been wallpapered once, in the 1930s, and had probably only been used as a storeroom after that.

Peeling back the wallpaper in other rooms

gave a clear idea of when the redecoration had taken place. The kitchen walls still had their original varnish paper as a bottom layer and a 1950s pattern was the most recent. Maxine counted six layers of wallpaper in the hallway and felt that when she removed them she was stripping away the past and that it was now their turn to make their mark on the house.

LEFT *The house as it looked when the Walshes first saw it.*

ABOVE *The new front door was a labour of love that immediately transformed the exterior. The somewhat dilapidated dormer window has been replaced by a Velux roof light, while new curtains and a glow from the stained glass make the house look like home.*

planning and preparation

two

RIGHT *A beautifully restored, wood-panelled Georgian room, with a deep cornice and two-part window shutters. Careful planning and attention to detail are essential when decorating a room like this, but the rewards are obvious.*

Careful planning and preparation are vital. They are the keys to the success of any home restoration project, so don't be tempted to skip this chapter in favour of more exciting, hands-on information. Proper planning and preparation will save you time, money and, possibly, your sanity.

Preliminary planning

Assuming that you have recently bought a house in need of restoration, you may already have some idea of the work that needs doing immediately, because a structural survey will have been a mortgage requirement. This will, however, have been done primarily to establish the value of the property rather than its condition. If the house has not been surveyed recently and you intend to embark on a major programme of decoration, you would be well advised to employ a building surveyor and obtain a full report, including his estimation of the possible costs of any structural work that needs doing. If you have a Conservation Officer on the local borough council, make an appointment for him or her to visit the house and carry out an inspection as well. They should do this regardless of whether or not you intend to apply for a grant, although they will be able to advise you on which areas of the renovation would qualify, and what your chances would be of getting approval. Conservation Officers are there to help, so make friends with them and see them as allies rather than bureaucrats, and you may find that they can unofficially recommend all the best local people to handle the restoration work.

It is best not to concentrate on the financial side at this stage, but to get as clear a picture as possible of what it is that you want to do to the house. Begin by noting down everything that you know needs doing: the major changes that would make the house best suited to your needs (e.g. bigger kitchen, central heating, skylight windows); the features that you would like to put back (e.g. fireplaces, panel doors, stained glass, floor tiles); and the way you would like to decorate the house, including the floor coverings, window treatments, lighting and wall finishes you most want.

Make a room-by-room inspection, writing down your requirements for each one as you go. This will help you to see the whole picture and decide on your priorities. Remember that your life is going to be turned upside-down when you let the builders in and staggering the operation could be a way of getting some breathing space. This would also mean that the financing could be less crippling.

Put a file together that contains all the relevant information, plus any photographs, cuttings, drawings or articles that you think will help explain your intentions and prepare for the next stage.

Architects

There is no doubt that an architect will be helpful on all but the most straightforward of jobs, particularly if the project involves the overseeing of people with different skills, such as bricklayers, electricians, plasterers and plumbers. Architects also know about Building Regulations and planning permission, safety issues and which grants you could be eligible for. Conservation architects specialize in restoration work and are sensitive to the special requirements of old buildings. The Royal

Architects' fees can be high. They charge either a percentage of the whole contract or an hourly rate. It is important to establish the cost of their services right from the start, so that you don't get a nasty shock later on. If money is very tight you could use an architect just in the early stages – for advice and to draw up any plans you need.

Make sure that you communicate your ideas and wishes as precisely and comprehensively as you can. If necessary, ask for clear explanations and reasons if, eventually, there are any departures from them. You can reasonably expect your architect to:

- attend an initial discussion meeting on or off site;
- develop sketches of different treatments;
- provide detailed plans and drawings;
- submit applications for Building Regulations Approval or planning permission;
- know which grants are available and how to apply for them;
- know which builders specialize in restoration work;
- prepare the contracts and monitor the work.

A conservation architect will also know about the use of traditional materials to repair old buildings and have contact with craftsmen who specialize in areas such as plasterwork, wood carving, stained glass and thatching.

If you just need to have a drawing done (to submit for Building Regulations Approval) then you could use the services of an architectural technician, who will have BTEC (British Technical Education Certificate) qualifications and be able to draw plans to the required standard. Find one locally by contacting the

Institute of British Architects (RIBA) produces a leaflet explaining specialist areas. It is called *From Cottages to Cathedrals – how a conservation architect can help you* and is available from RIBA (see page 186), which will also be able to provide names of local conservation architects on request.

You can make an appointment to see an architect for an initial 'fact finding' meeting, with no obligation to proceed. Arrange to meet on site if possible, so that you can show the architect exactly what you mean and he or she can inspect the house at the same time and see the pitfalls and the potential. Initial meetings usually last an hour and may be free of charge, but you should check this when you make the appointment. Architects tackle jobs of all sizes, so don't imagine that yours will be too small for them to consider. Their input can make a particularly important contribution to your planning stages, and they will often be able to suggest solutions to problems that thought were insurmountable.

THE HOME FRONT GUIDE

British Institute of Architectural Technologists (BIAT, see page 186).

Surveyors

Of the different types of surveyor, the one that will concern you here is the building surveyor whose special area is dealing with the repair, alteration, extension and restoration of existing buildings. Choose a chartered building surveyor with the letters RICS or FRICS after his or her name, which means that they are members or fellows of the Royal Institute of Chartered Surveyors. They will be able to:

- conduct a survey;
- provide drawings for official consents;
- make sketched drawings of the proposed alterations;
- apply for planning permission and Building Regulations Approval;
- estimate the cost of the work;
- put the job out to tender and oversee the work's progress.

So they replace the need for an architect if no new design work is involved. They are generally less expensive to employ than an architect, and work on a fixed fee, hourly rate or percentage of the contract and it is up to you to agree terms for payment. The initial meeting should not be charged for, but make sure that you fully understand the costs from that point on, and have a written agreement.

Planning permission

You need to apply for planning permission from the local council for certain types of improvements and any changes that will alter the look of your house from the outside. These would include things such as adding a front or side extension; converting the house into flats; converting an outbuilding into living space;

erecting a solid garden wall of above-average height; rebuilding part of the house; or doing anything at all to a listed building.

You are permitted to extend your house if it has no existing extension and if the new building will not be visible from the street, but only if you keep the extension within 70 cubic metres for most houses, and 50 cubic metres if the house terraced, if it is in a Conservation Area, National Park or a designated Area of Outstanding Natural Beauty.

You will need to submit proof that you actually own the property, a location map, technical drawings, and details of the materials that you intend using. You also need to show how access will be gained (will your builders obstruct a shared alleyway, for instance, or go through a neighbour's garden?). You will need to have the drawings done by a professional – a surveyor, an architectural technician or an architect. Your application is submitted to the planning office of the local borough council and you will be given their decision within eight weeks. They either approve, approve with conditions attached, or disapprove. If neighbours object, there could be delays of up to six months, or even longer. You can appeal against their refusal and there is a booklet called *Planning Appeals* that explains the procedure. Published by the Department of the Environment, it is available from council offices.

Never be tempted to start work without permission, or to carry on despite a refusal; there are penalties and you will be required to remove the new addition as well as pay a fine.

Listed Building Consent

If your house is a listed building you will need Listed Building Consent in addition to planning permission for any external or internal work that affects the character of the building. The

local council will be able to tell you whether your house is listed. If it was built before 1700, then it will be; if between 1700 and 1840, then it is likely to be; if between 1840 and 1914 and of distinctive quality and character, then it may be; and if built after that, it would have to be of unique architectural style, or of special architectural interest, to be listed.

Building Regulations Approval

It is important to realize that this is quite a separate matter from obtaining planning permission, and getting one does not mean that you do not have to get the other. These regulations are about certain standards that all building work must conform to. They exist for our safety as much as anything else and are very strictly enforced. As with a lot of legislation, the actual Building Regulations would be impossible for a lay person to understand, but shortened, simplified versions are available from your local council and their Building Inspector will be happy to visit and advise you on whether or not you need apply.

LEFT *The removal of a dividing wall to open up a large living space – to make a kitchen/dining and living room as seen here, for example – is a job that needs properly drawn plans and Building Regulations Approval.*

drawings before the work starts. There are fees that vary according to the scale of the project. If the plans are passed, you will be notified and possibly sent Building Regulations Inspection Cards; these must be sent back at stages during the work to allow the inspector a chance to visit the site and check the work. Hand them to your builder.

2. You can simply notify the council by means of a Building Notice Approval Form. You do not make an application but inform them of what you are doing and they are free to inspect at any time.

The second option is the more suitable for small jobs, where there is unlikely to be any conflict with the regulations. On a bigger, more expensive job there is always a risk that an inspector may object and ask for the work to be redone, or he or she may not feel that enough has been done and you could find your costs escalating. At least with an approval you will know from the start what needs doing and be able to budget accordingly.

Tempting though it may be to get stuck straight into your house's restoration, there is nothing to be gained and a lot to be lost from failing to obtain official approval. You may find that you get useful information from the Building Inspector. His job will have brought him into contact with other people with similar houses in the area, and knowing something of their restoration experiences could be very helpful.

Drawing your own plans

If you do not want to make any major structural alterations and feel that you do not need the services of either an architect or a surveyor, it will help your decision making if you

The type of work that is likely to need approval is: the removal or part removal of a supporting wall; insulation of a cavity wall; underpinning; connecting a service – such as water, gas or electricity; adding an extension or putting in French windows. Your architect, surveyor and builder will know exactly what work is subject to Building Regulations Approval.

You can deal with obtaining approval in two different ways:

1. Submit full plans with a set of technical

make a careful ground plan of all the rooms in the house. If you work to scale you can use the drawings to plan your central heating and lighting circuits, and also to brief your builders. Include all the doors and windows and the main furniture items, and note the space needed for opening doors and drawers. Place tracing paper overlays on each room plan and use these to plot the positions of central-heating radiators, and also the light fittings and electrical plugs.

Central heating

If you decide to install central heating, give it a good deal of thought and get as much advice as you can. The National Heating Consultancy (NHC, see page 186) operates a free telephone advice line and will provide you with enough information to be able to relay your requirements to a heating engineer, using the right technical jargon. For a fee, they will also send an expert to visit you to advise on the best and most economical heating system to suit your house and your lifestyle.

Think about running costs: a three-storey house, for instance, could, for little extra cost, have a set of controls on each floor allowing you to heat only the rooms in use while just keeping the chill off those that are not. The NHC advises using two boilers in a large house, a small one to handle a third of the house's requirements and a bigger one to deal with the other two-thirds. The small one can be used when just hot water is needed, the larger one during an average winter, and both together in extremely cold conditions.

They offer two general tips; to site radiators under windows when possible – because there they will heat cool air as it enters, whereas on internal walls the heat will simply rise to the ceiling; and to site shelves 5–7cm above radiators, with a good seal on the wall, so that hot air is pushed out to the front.

If you feel that new radiators would look too intrusively modern, you could either disguise them by boxing them in, or consider buying the old, elaborate column-style ones. While the design is not as heat-efficient as the modern radiators, they do have a wonderfully solid presence. General architectural salvage yards usually have a stock of old radiators, but check them over for cracks and metal fatigue before you buy them. If they have been left filled and the water has frozen at some point, the cast iron may have cracked. There are also several firms that specialize in restoring old radiators; these will give you a choice of different patterns and the reassurance of knowing they are fit for use. New reproduction ones, in a variety of finishes including stoved enamel in a range of colours, are also available.

Lighting

The wiring in any old house should be professionally checked because standards for wiring, fittings and appliances have changed over the years and old wiring can be dangerous. Use an electrician registered with the National Inspection Council for Electrical Installation Contracting (NICEIC, see page 186) and who has experience of working on old buildings.

If you are having the house re-wired then this is the time to plan the position of plugs, wall lights, special circuits, dimmer switches and recessed ceiling spotlights. Even though its full effect will not be seen until the rooms have been decorated and furnished, lighting should be considered at an early stage, because any new wiring needs to be done before plastering. This is particularly important for wall lights because, while you can conceal wall fittings behind pictures until you find the right lights, you cannot add wall lights without replastering and redecorating. Think carefully about your planned furniture layout, and if you are likely to change rooms around a lot, try to find flexible lighting solutions.

Scaled drawings of your room plans will be doubly useful: not only will your instructions be perfectly clear but, once the work is done, your electrician can draw in the position of the cabling so that you never have the shock (literally) of banging a nail into concealed wiring.

If you are lucky enough to find old light fittings that suit your house style, it is vital to have them re-wired and brought up to current safety standards by a lighting specialist. Reconditioned lights are available from specialist dealers and a lot of antique-style lighting is now being reproduced. A period house can also be lit by concealed lighting. Small halogen uplighters and spots can wash the walls with gentle light and highlight treasures.

Builders

If you do not already know a good builder, choose one who has done good work for close friends. Personal experience is worth a lot more than glossy advertising, and someone who approaches an old building with care and sensitivity is worth their weight in gold.

The selection process will be easier if you are working within a Conservation Area, because you will be able to ask neighbours for recommendations, and the Conservation Officer will almost certainly be able, unofficially, to recommend a local builder who undertakes restoration work. The architect or surveyor who drew up your plans may also be able to introduce you to the right person.

If you are stuck, it is worth asking a national organization like the Federation of Master Builders to provide names of local builders who specialize in old buildings. The Scottish Building Employers' Federation or the Building Employers' Confederation are also worth approaching.

If your house is a very old building, you should employ a specialist and the Society for the Protection of Ancient Buildings (see page 186) will help you to find the right person.

Consider how long the work is going to take, and whether or not you will be living on site during the upheaval. You may have to be in close contact with the builder for a few months and it is important that you are able to get along. Someone might possess the most impressive qualifications but if they are unsympathetic to your wishes, scratch them off the list.

Obtaining a quotation

Always ask for a quotation, not an estimate; the first states the price, the second just gives a rough idea. You will need to invite three or four contractors to submit quotes for the work. For these to be realistic, you need to draw up a job specification that is as clear as possible and includes any special conditions that you would like to apply.

You will also need a quote for the cost of the preparation work involved, such as clearing out the old materials and burning off old paint, or perhaps scaffolding the building.

Make a detailed list of all the work that needs doing, divided up into External and Internal categories. For example:

External
- Repair damage to roof using original-style slates.
- Repair section of guttering above the side bay window using original-style (not plastic) replacement.
- Repoint west-facing wall as necessary, with a matching render.

- Replace rotten sash windows in front bay with new ones in same style.

Internal

Front Reception Room
- Replace rotten floorboarding with reclaimed boards of a similar style.
- Install reconditioned fireplace and re-tile.
- Replaster section of wall above the doorway.

Entrance Hall
- Restore brickwork surrounding the front door and replaster.
- Fit replacement dado rail to match existing section.

And so on ... The most important thing is to be as specific as possible. Do not worry about using the correct terminology, just explain clearly what you want; and do ask the builder whether he is unsure about anything that you have included on your list .

Once you have accepted a quotation, specify when you would like the work to begin and ask for a firm commitment to a completion date. Be prepared, however, for this to change if unexpected problems, like dry rot under floorboards, are discovered.

Safeguards and contracts

Ask about the builder's insurance cover, guarantees offered and how long they last, and inform the builder that you will be issuing a written contract. There are various contracts that cover this sort of work, and you can buy them from RIBA or The Building Centre Bookshop (see page 186). The agreement for Minor Building Works is suitable for a small job where you have not involved an architect but wish to have a legally binding contract between yourself and the builder. If you get a renovation grant then you will need an RG(C) Agreement for Renovation Grant Works if you are not

using an architect, or an RG(A) Agreement if you are using one.

State your payment schedule in the contract, making it staggered, rather than in a lump sum, with a final payment withheld for a period after completion, to give time to check that the work has been properly done.

As an addendum to the contract, it is also worth stipulating that minimal local disruption should be caused by the parking of vehicles and siting of skips and materials. (Think of the neighbours.)

If the building work is minor, or if you feel that the builder would be reluctant to wade through the paperwork, then you can just draw up a letter of contract. This should include detailed specifications of the work (install the new bathroom fixtures, for example), the starting and completion dates, the price and the payment arrangements and any guarantees involved. This is also in the interest of the builder, to prevent any misunderstanding later on.

There is a good book published by the Consumers' Association in the form of a *Which?* guide, called *Getting Work Done on Your House*, which covers all aspects of contracts, permissions and employing professionals.

Survival techniques

If you are having major structural repair work done you will need a bolt-hole, some neutral territory where you have the peace and tranquillity that existed before the hammering, drilling, transistor radios and concrete-mixing began. Ideally, you would live somewhere nearby, to keep an eye on things but also be able to escape. A lot of people have been

THE MUNICIPAL
BATH & WASH-HOUSE

OPENING HOURS

FOR MEN:

FOR WOMEN:

known to spend over a year as 'garden gypsies' while doing the building work themselves in the evenings and at weekends. One woman had her first baby soon after taking up residence in the caravan and was still there two years later when her twins were on the way. The reward for her forbearance was a beautifully hand-restored fifteenth-century house – and, happily, a very close family unit.

If you decide to take the mobile-home option and employ a builder to do the work, make sure he finishes the bathroom or shower and toilet first because these are the facilities that you will miss the most. One family who were renovating a large London house from scratch on their own actually completed a very luxurious bathroom in the midst of total chaos. It had a family-sized bath, an open fire and fitted carpets. After their day on the building site the parents would gather up their two small children, light the fire and wallow together in luxury – the perfect restorative! Theirs was admittedly an extreme solution, but the ideology is worth thinking about. It is important not to sacrifice too much of the present as an investment in the future. You are far more likely to enjoy the restoration process if you feel in control, although there are bound to be times when it looks like a bewildering, unmanageable mess. If you watched Graham and Maxine Walsh on *Home Front* you will know that the house they took possession of looked quite solid and well kept until they began ripping up floorboards, knocking out bits of wall and stripping the wallpaper. They admitted feeling that no progress was being made at all, but then quite suddenly the 'first fix' was over and the house was re-wired, centrally heated and the decoration was underway.

The Walshes stayed in their rented house as long as possible, but you may have to live in while the work is being done. Most people find that they can manage quite well, but you need to be as organized as possible. If the house is big enough, set up a kitchen and living room in one bedroom. A Calor Gas stove, rented from a camping supplier's, and a microwave oven will be invaluable. The more space you can allow the builders to occupy, the faster the work will proceed, so if possible stay right out of the way. Move everything breakable, valuable or likely to get in their way into the room that needs the least amount of work doing. It is a good idea to do all this type of preparation before any work starts, then the builders can get straight down to the job.

Discuss toilet and tea-making arrangements before they begin. It may seem petty but these are the things that can drive you mad. If there is just one loo, upstairs, then you could reasonably ask them to bring a portaloo, and be specific about where they put it – remember the neighbours. Find out if the builder has a mobile phone and, if not, make clear rules about the use of your own line, i.e. only calls relating to your own building work.

Noise can be very stressful, so try to discover when the neighbours are least likely to object and arrange for the loudest jobs to be done during those times. It is also worth making it clear from the start that you would rather they did not work to the accompaniment of radios turned on at full blast.

If the work that they are doing is dependent upon good weather, try to have alternative jobs for them to be getting on with if the weather turns bad. Don't allow your living areas to become their immediate refuge in case of sudden showers. And, a final caveat, try to control your inclination to 'chat' and be chummy; the time it takes is literally at your expense, so keep work and play separate. It really is not important whether or not the builder likes you, but good communication and respect for each other are.

A good builder is invaluable and will most likely have foreseen all these eventualities and more. Give him time to reveal his sensitive side before wading in with a list of do's and don'ts – you may be pleasantly surprised.

Finances

Somewhere along the line you will have begun to get an inkling of the cost of the work that you propose doing. Friends are always keen to cost the job for you, based on what their builder charged for something similar five years ago. Listen to them with half an ear, but also consult consumer publications like the *Which?* guides, and pay special attention to anyone who has had work done on a period property. It is much easier to underestimate the cost than to overestimate, so prepare yourself for a shock when you get the builder's quotation.

This is where your initial groundwork comes in handy. You need to separate the essential from non-essential work and generally prioritize your list according to the cost of the work. The builder may be able to suggest areas where he sees potential for savings, especially with regard to your choice of materials. You may be unfamiliar with new technology and distrust its suitability; if so, ask the Conservation Officer or a traditional building expert whether or not it would be suitable. If new materials are invisible, cost less, and will not affect the character of your house, then they are worth considering. Architectural salvage yards can provide the authentic materials that you need, but they can also be expensive. Cost all the items that you intend to buy from them, as well as all their compatible fixtures and fittings, before adding up the figures for the building work.

As a rough estimate the building work should cost 75 per cent of the whole job. The architect, architectural technician or building surveyor will cost between 10 per cent and 14 per cent and the local authority permissions 1 per cent. You should also keep 10 per cent back for unexpected costs (discovery of rot or infestation when floorboards are lifted, etc.).

Budgeting

Unless you have a bulging bank account, you will have to raise the money to do the work. If you have savings to draw upon, it is worth remembering that a cheque will provide a traceable record of the payment, but on the other hand, if you offer ready cash for small jobs, you may be able to negotiate a discount (but be sure to count out the money in front of the recipient).

Personal Loans

A bank loan is one possibility, and you should make an appointment to see the Lending Officer of your bank, taking all the plans and estimates along with you. They will need to be convinced of your ability to repay over a certain time and will charge the going rate for a Personal Loan.

Adding to an existing mortgage

You need to ask your mortgage lender for a Home Improvement Loan to cover the cost of the restoration work. If they agree, the new repayment will be added on to your present repayment. This may be the most painless way of doing things. You need to know what the market value of your property is and whether the improvements will increase its value enough to cover the loan. If this is not the case, the mortgage company will require you to take out an insurance policy to cover the difference.

Taking out a second mortgage

This means borrowing from a new source. Check the company's credentials before accepting any apparently attractive offers. They should be members of the Finance and Leasing Association, and it is best to stick to reputable, established lenders.

When you borrow money at a low interest rate, you must allow for increases when making financial projections. A sharp rise in interest rates can be crippling if you are paying back a large amount or two separate loans. So don't be tempted to go for as much as you can get; try and stick with the lowest possible amount.

Grants

Never assume that you will automatically get a grant, because all grants are governed by cash flow, and there is only a limited amount of money available. And though the council may agree that you are eligible for assistance, if there are a hundred other applications already being processed you may have to join the queue. The problem this poses is that no work can begin until the council gives you the go-ahead, and this could take time. If you can afford to do so, budget to pay for all the work yourself, especially the essential structural repairs, then approach the relevant grant departments to see what you might be eligible for and put in an application. In this way you will be able to treat any grant you get as a windfall that can be ploughed back into your house's restoration.

Renovation grants

If you have bought a house that has no inside toilet, or needs plumbing, floors, windows, etc. before it can be habitable, and you are willing to be means-tested by the local authority, there is a chance that you will get a renovation grant (from the Environmental Health Department) to bring your home into line with accepted standards. There is a very clear and understandable booklet on this type of grant, published by the Department of the Environment and available from your local borough council office. Called *House Renovation Grants*, it will tell you all you need to know.

Architectural grants

These grants, issued by the Technical Services/ Conservation Department of your borough council, are intended to help keep work done on historically or architecturally interesting buildings 'in character'. The grant covers a percentage of the cost of the work, and you need to involve your local Conservation Officer (if you are lucky enough to have one in the area) or the local Technical Services Department from the word go. The areas of work that qualify for this type of grant include: slate roofs; clay tiles; chimney pots; lead flashing; repairs to cornices or mouldings; replacement of windows in the original style; repairs to balconies, railings or balustrades. Financial help may also possibly be available towards professional fees, scaffolding and VAT.

Ask your local borough council office for a leaflet explaining the conditions and requirements for eligibility. It is not a means-tested grant but the supply of money for this excellent cause is bound to be limited, so set the wheels in motion immediately.

Conservation Area partnership grant

This is an Area Targeted Grant issued by the Technical Services Department of the local borough council in partnership with English Heritage. English Heritage have recognized that there are certain areas with buildings of particular historic and architectural interest which have fallen into disrepair because the local economy has slumped. They have also recognized that the upkeep of these buildings is a matter of national importance and allocated sums of money to be used to restore them. The grants are available to listed buildings and other buildings of character and historic interest that lie within local Conservation Areas. They cover 40 per cent of the cost of the work and are intended to help towards the greater costs involved in getting high-quality repairs done using traditional materials and methods. The sort of work that is covered would include the restoration of lost architectural features like balconies, windows, doors and railings, or typical features such as weatherboarding or hung tilework. These grants are not means-tested because the area as a whole has already been designated to receive this assistance.

Other sources of grant aid

Your local council offices will be able to give you details of any other local schemes that operate, and it is worth making the effort to speak to both the Environmental and Technical Services Departments, because in some cases the latter are willing to top up an amenity grant with an architectural grant to make sure that essential repairwork to an old building is sympathetically carried out.

RIGHT *Matchboarding, also known as tongue-and-groove panelling, was used a lot in small Victorian and Edwardian houses, especially in the country and in attic bedrooms. It is readily available in kit form. The hinged curtain rods are a good solution for small dormer windows, allowing maximum light in during the day, and not concealing the pretty Gothic window shapes.*

THE WALSHES' PLANNING EXPERIENCE

The Walshes had three jobs that needed official Building Regulations Approval: the partial demolition of a wall between the kitchen and dining room, the removal of the chimney breast in the bathroom, and the replacement of the dormer with a Velux window in the loft. This third job also needed planning permission.

The Walshes asked an architect, Suzanne White, for some help, and felt that her fee was well worth it. She explored all the options for combining the kitchen and dining room and, when they had come to a decision, drew up the plans that were needed; she then applied for, and obtained, official approval for all three jobs at the same time. Each separate application involves the payment of a fee, so it was a good idea to sort out all the jobs that might need Building Regulations Approval and planning permission and submit one application for the lot, in order to save money.

Graham and his father, who had previous building experience, felt confident enough to tackle the demolition of the wall themselves, working to the architect's specifications, and it was a great success.

The well-known interior designer Kevin McCloud visited the Walshes when they were still in the planning stages of their restoration work, and advised them on the best way to light their home. He explained on *Home Front* that lighting falls into five main categories: ambient – all-round light; accent – to highlight particular features; task – to throw light on worktops, desks, etc.; decorative – a lamp as an ornament; and kinetic – moving, flickering candlelight. The different kinds can be combined in various ways to make the best use of a room, and to show its features off to best advantage. To help the Walshes visualize light effects, he used torches and car inspection lamps to simulate the effect of up- and downlighters, spotlights or concealed lights. He introduced them to the idea of a lighting circuit in the living room. This makes it possible for all the lamps to be switched on, off or dimmed from one wall-mounted switch, yet still be operated individually. He also suggested using recessed halogen ceiling spots on the stairs. Three of these small lights provide all the light needed for both stairs and hallway, and the Walshes liked the effect so much that they are using it for the kitchen as well. (These are not suitable for use in all old buildings, so check with an electrician before you invest in them.) He also advised them to light the front steps with one or two lanterns, to provide a welcome for visitors.

LEFT *The freshly opened-up wall, showing the RSJ that was inserted to support the wall above the opening.*

BELOW *The finished wall with its custom-made ash plate-rack, rich-coloured wallpaper and a glimpse of the restored kitchen range. Employing an architect helped the Walshes to choose the very best solution for connecting the kitchen and dining room.*

exteriors

he exterior of a period house should retain as much of its original character as possible. Think of the front of the house as a mature face, with the windows and front door as the features, the brickwork or render as the skin and the roof as its crowning glory. In the same way that an older face loses its dignity when disfigured with too much make-up and an unnaturally youthful hairstyle, so a house is seldom improved by exterior modernization.

Many of the problems that plague old buildings are the result of unsympathetic alterations and repairs. For example, something as simple as a coating of water-repellent masonry paint can create rather than cure damp, especially if the internal walls have been painted with washable vinyl paint. It is like making a damp sandwich – the moisture has nowhere to go and the rot sets in, literally. Windows and doors should always be repaired or replaced with exact copies of the originals. If you need convincing, take a look at any old house fitted with new aluminium or UPVC windows and a 'Georgian-style' front door with a built-in fanlight; then find a similar house with its original features intact. There is no contest – the originals look solid, comfortable and harmonious, the replacements look flimsy and all too obviously fake.

Roofing

Once you start to notice roofing materials and detailing you will realize how important the style is to the look of the whole house. Fired clay tiles or Welsh slates fit the house like a tailored suit, hugging the curves and flattering the shape. Modern concrete tiles have a cumbersome regular shape and a typically flat, unvarying colour. So beware of the hard-sell roofer who tries to convince you to replace your original tiles with a cheaper concrete

version. Not only do they look less attractive, but they also weigh considerably more and your roof structure may not be strong enough to support them. An independent expert – either an architect, a structural engineer or a building surveyor – should assess the roof timbers before you even consider concrete. If you have to renew a slate roof, you could consider using some of the 'fake' slate tiles that are now on the market. But again, beware: they vary in appearance, price and quality. The best are made from crushed Welsh slate bound into a resin and moulded from original slates; they age naturally, are lightweight and carry a sixty-year guarantee. The less expensive ones tend to look too regular in colour, shape and texture, and so are far less appropriate for a period house. You may be shocked at the price of second-hand clay tiles or slates, but try to think of your roof as a valuable commodity that has an appreciating resale value.

Roof tiles are laid in different ways. Most flat tiles are double lapped, which means that they are overlapped and staggered; shaped, interlocking tiles can be single lapped, which means that they are not staggered, making them more economical because fewer tiles are used and they are easier to lay.

Ridge tiles

Ridge tiles can add a very decorative finishing touch to a roof. Look at roofs in the neighbourhood; if some have fancy clay ridge tiles, it would be worth visiting a local architectural salvage yard to find some in a

similar style. Detailing like this enhances the whole area, as well as your house.

Flat roofs

If you have an old house with a flat roof, it is likely to have had an original covering of sheet metal – copper, lead or zinc. These materials are still used by restoration experts but asphalt is a cheaper and acceptable alternative. It is laid in two hot coats then scattered with heat-reflective limestone chippings to prevent it distorting on hot days. To be effective, asphalt should be laid by experts, so use a reputable company to do any necessary work. One big advantage of this material is that it can be patched by cutting out the damage and pouring on molten asphalt – once again, a job for the experts.

Thatch

Thatching has always been done according to local traditional patterns. Find your nearest thatcher by contacting the National Council of Master Thatchers Associations (see page 186), which will give recommendations and advice on all aspects of thatching.

Flashings

Flashings are the lead strips used to seal junctions between roof tiles and chimneys or abutting walls. Lead does deteriorate and flashings should be regularly inspected – and suspected – if you have signs of leaking. You need a metal roof specialist to carry out repairs.

Walls

Conservation experts all agree that you should repair like with like – using the same type of materials that the house is made from, not their modern equivalents. This may mean buying second-hand bricks from an architectural

LEFT **Each of these two semi-detached houses has undergone some modernization. The one on the left retains its true period character despite being painted because it still has the original windows, front door and finialled gable. The other house has been robbed of all these and looks drab and featureless.**

REPLACING A BRICK

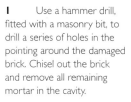

1   Use a hammer drill, fitted with a masonry bit, to drill a series of holes in the pointing around the damaged brick. Chisel out the brick and remove all remaining mortar in the cavity.

2   Coat the edges of the replacement brick with new mortar and slide it into the cavity. Finish off the repair by matching the pointing to the rest of the wall.

salvage yard or searching for a builder who knows about lime mortar. If the costs of doing the job properly are way out of your intended budget, talk to your local Conservation Officer; he or she may be able to suggest areas where savings could be made by using new materials unobtrusively, and may even offer you a grant to pay for the extra costs.

Lime was 'rediscovered' during the 1980s when distressed paint finishes, such as rag rolling, became so popular. The resurgence of interest in limed oak, limewash and distemper finishes regenerated an interest in lime as a building material. This previously very specialized area has opened up enormously as the message started to get through that lime putty – the active ingredient used in making old plaster, mortar and paint – has very desirable qualities that differ from those of the modern equivalents. One of these is flexibility – it allows a building to move slightly without cracking up and the other is its ability to absorb and release

moisture – in effect, it breathes. Portland cement, which was first patented in 1824, replaced the lime in mortar; gypsum replaced it in plaster; and plastic replaced it in paint – and when these new materials are used to repair the originals, problems can arise. If your house was built in the early nineteenth century, ask your builder what he knows about lime before he starts. For more information about lime, contact the Lime Centre (see page 186).

Brickwork

If your house is built with bricks, check the pointing – that is, the mortar around them. The walls need re-pointing if there are spaces where mortar should be. Take note of the style of pointing that has been used elsewhere and try to copy it. Basically, the mortar will either be flush with the brick face or rebated, but there are variations in the style. A bit of flattery goes a long way, and most bricklayers will see the job as a challenge and a chance to exhibit their skill.

1   A small crack can be repaired with exterior filler. Tap around the area with a trowel handle. Any render that sounds hollow should be removed. Only where it sounds solid is the render secure.

2   Using a cold chisel and hammer, carefully chip away the damaged render. Make the repair neat and manageable by chipping away a roughly regular rectangular shape.

3   Use a wire brush to clean up the brick surface, dust it, and then wet it down with a soft brush.

4   Use proprietary exterior filler or make up render using 1 part cement to 3 parts sand mixed with 1 part PVA diluted with 3 parts water. Apply two thin coats rather than just one thick coat. When dry, sand and repaint.

If you want to do the re-pointing yourself, start in the least conspicuous place – it is not as easy as you think.

If any of the bricks have 'spalled' (crumbled away) then they should be removed and replaced. It is possible to do this yourself by following the step-by-step guide on page 43.

The chances are that you will be able to find second-hand matching bricks at your local salvage yard. If you need a particular type of brick that is difficult to find, it is possible to get one from a company that specializes in hand-made bricks. You can find one by looking in the SALVO information sheets (see page 186).

Pay particular attention to the window and door arches; these must kept in good repair or the rest of the building will be affected. Arches are made from specially tapered bricks with a central keystone, and the opening is supported by a hidden lintel. If an arch starts to collapse, the lintel may need replacing, or the wall may be sinking because of a problem with the building's foundations. A surveyor's report will pinpoint the fault, and it is essential to deal with it properly and not do just a cosmetic repair.

Stucco

This is a weatherproof plaster coating that was widely used during the late eighteenth and nineteenth centuries. It allowed the builders to conceal poor-quality brickwork – acting like a thick coat of icing does on a less than perfect cake. Georgian houses often had their whole façades covered, but Victorian builders tended to use it decoratively to dress up windows, doorways and add decorative grandeur with string courses and cornices. Stucco details like mouldings give a building its character and so, even if they are damaged, they should be retained and repaired rather than chipped away.

A crack or small hole in a flat area of stucco can be repaired by following our step-by-step guide opposite. Anything larger needs the help of an expert, as two different coats of render are needed. If you leave damaged stucco unrepaired, water may seep underneath and cause damp problems. If an area is bulging or bowing out, it means that it has already been damaged by damp, and needs hacking off and patching with new render. A cornice has to be repaired *in situ*, using a running mould. You will need to find an expert to do the work; your council Conservation Officer may know of one locally.

Roughcast and pebble dash

These finishes were popular in the late Victorian and Edwardian periods. Rough sand is mixed into the render to give the textured finish of roughcast, and pebbles are flicked into the surface of the render and bedded in before it dries to give the pebble-dash effect. Repairs should be done in the same way after chipping away all the damaged area.

Stonework

Although we tend to think of stone as strong and permanent, it is, sadly, as prone to corrosion by pollution as other materials. If you compare the rural stone houses of the Cotswolds with those in the industrial cities in the North, you can see the blackening effect of smoking chimneys. Now acid rain is beginning to have an effect, eating away the surface and reducing fine details to blurred outlines.

Stone has always been an expensive building material, but was used well into this century to add strength and decoration around windows and doorways. Coping stones were used to top off brick walls, and protruding stone courses were added, sometimes in the form of architraves and cornices, because quite apart from looking good, they shed water, protecting the brickwork.

Damaged stone needs professional care. In areas where stone is readily available, local builders will be familiar with its treatment; in other areas ask the local Conservation Officer for advice. Because of the expense of replacing damaged stone, it is more likely to be repaired with pins and mortar. The stone is drilled, then pins or a wire framework are glued in, to give the mortar a good grip.

Cracks in the walls

Small, stable cracks are not a cause for worry, and they can be filled. New cracks need attention. There are several reasons why a building may begin to crack. The soil below is often the culprit, especially in times of drought. Water drains out of the clay-based soil, causing it to sink; luckily, when the soil regains its normal moisture, cracks often correct themselves. If the house stands on sandstone the problems can get worse when rain finally falls, because sand tends to be eroded rather than reconstituted. The good news is that all this type of work will be covered by your building insurance. Get a building surveyor to report on and supervise the work.

Trees that are too close to the walls may also cause cracking. A tree sucks a huge amount of water from the ground and this can be exacerbated by the spread of its roots, which can be phenomenal – a poplar's roots spread wider than its height. It is not advisable to remove an established tree (they are likely to be protected by law anyway) because the soil may flood where it was previously drained, causing even more problems. Trees should be controlled by lopping, which must be done by a tree surgeon.

Overloading a house may also cause problems. If the beams were designed to carry a certain weight, they may not be able to take the strain of alterations and heavy new flooring, furniture and fixtures. A structural engineer or building surveyor will be the best judge of what your joists are capable of supporting.

Front doors

Our forebears certainly knew how to make an entrance. Front doors were made to impress, and each period, from Georgian to Edwardian, had its own style. With pediments and columns, ironwork arches, classical canopies or stained-glass windows, they reflected changing architectural fashions and also indicated what the interior style of the house might be. If your house has its original front door, you will be able to date it fairly accurately because the styles changed noticeably.

Typical door types

The following list is a rough guide to the main features of period front doors; it cannot possibly be comprehensive.

Georgian. Solid six-panelled door with fancy fanlight. Brass knocker but no letterplate.

Regency. Solid two-panelled door with fanlight. Simple door furniture, no letterplate but possibly a bell-pull.

Early Victorian. Panelled door with glazed panels above a central door knob and letterplate. Often a simple Gothic arch-shaped doorway. House number on brass plate, or individual numbers and possibly knocker and bell-pull.

Mid-Victorian. Large four-panelled door with ornate door surround, possibly with pediment, columns and swags of fruit and leaves. Fanlight. Decorative letter plate, door-pull bar, bell-pull and knocker.

Mid/late Victorian. Large panelled door

with three solid panels below and two large panels above topped by small glazed panels. Some with stained glass. Brass or iron letter plates, door-pulls, knockers, bell-pulls and numbers.

Queen Anne Revival. Many small, stained-glass panels in top half matched by many small solid wood panels below. Big door surround with glazed panels.

Arts and Crafts. Top third of the door glazed in panels. Some doors made of oak and left unpainted. Door surround includes glazed panels, canopy over door with wooden brackets. Black ironwork fittings.

Art Nouveau. Stained glass with narrow glazing bars. Curvilinear detailing. and fancy 'organic'-styled letterplate and numbers.

Edwardian. Three long solid panels topped with nine small glazed panels, sometimes set into oval shape. Large door surround with opening windows and some stained glass, and fretwork porches. Fanlights. Brass door fittings.

Most exterior doors of any period are either plank or panelled doors. Traditional plank doors are sometimes found as front doors of small country houses, old workers' cottages, or as back or outhouse doors in town houses. Towards the end of the nineteenth century the Arts and Crafts movement used plank doors with small glazed panels for their country-revival look, using oak instead of the usual painted pine.

A ledged plank door is made of a row of planks butted together with a cross-piece nailed across the top and bottom. A stronger version is ledged and braced, which means that it has two additional diagonal supporting struts; more complicated still is a ledged, braced and framed plank door, in which all the supports are surrounded by a frame. The fronts of these doors usually feature long wrought-iron strap

hinges but are otherwise quite plain, with all the bracing on the back.

If you have one of these doors it may be worth stripping off the layers of old paint and starting afresh. The grooves can become

ABOVE *The black iron fittings and railings are a perfect complement to this deep panelled mid-Victorian front door.*

Reproduction Exterior Door Furniture

1 **Rope scroll door knocker** (Georgian)
2 **Plain brass bell-push** (Georgian/Edwardian)
3 **Rope door knob** (Georgian)
4 **Brass ring knocker** (Georgian/early Victorian)
5 **Solid brass lion door knocker** (Victorian)
6 **Elegant brass numerals** (all periods)
7 **Centre door knob** (Late Georgian/early Victorian)
8 **Solid brass mechanical door-pull** (Victorian)
9 **Rope letterplate** (Georgian)
10 **Medusa door knocker** (Mid/late Victorian)
11 **Illuminated brass bell-push** (Victorian/Edwardian)
12 **Berlin black iron knocker** (Victorian)
13 **Brass letterplate** (Victorian)
14 **Black cast-iron letter plate** (Late Victorian)
15 **Bell push** (Georgian)
16 **Black cast-iron bell push** (Victorian)
17 **Berlin black iron door knocker** (Victorian/ Edwardian)

clogged with paint over the years and look much sharper once it has been removed. A job like this can be done with a hot-air stripper or chemical paint stripper (see page 75).

Panelled doors are still made in much the same way as they have been since they first appeared in the late eighteenth century. The only changes have been the number or arrangement of the panels, part glazing and the introduction of plywood in place of solid wood. Familiarity with the terminology and construction of a panelled door can be useful, either to help you put it back together if any of the joints have loosened, or if you need to describe possible repairs to a carpenter. Two vertical stiles and at least three cross-rails provide the basic frame. The vertical pieces that divide the panels within the frame are called muntins. The panels fit into the grooves in the frame and the joins are usually covered with mitred mouldings. The door is held together by mortise-and-tenon joints – a male/female arrangement – that are glued together, but the panels are held in the frame without glue, to avoid the wood splitting if shrinkage occurs.

Glazed panels in the doors themselves, sometimes surrounded by glazed side-panels and fanlights, were introduced during the nineteenth century. They allowed more light into dark hallways and also offered opportunities for more decoration in the form of stained glass. Fanlights above the front door became very decorative during the Georgian era, with fancy metalwork, or carved wooden glazing bars radiating out into the semi-circular shape. Later on these were replaced by rectangular, clear or stained-glass panels that sometimes featured the number of the house. Stained-glass windows were an essential element of the Gothic Revival style, and the idea was taken up and used in different forms

by the Arts and Crafts movement and later by the Queen Anne Revival movement, and remained popular throughout the first half of this century in various styles.

The original front door would have been made to suit the character of your house; its proportions carefully considered and the decorative elements designed in keeping with the style of the building. So it is always worth trying to save – even when it seems to be falling to pieces. The cost of having a replica door made by a skilled joiner would be far higher than having the original repaired. SPAB runs an informal advice line and will refer you to skilled craftsmen (see page 186). The sheer quality of the old wood is another reason to restore rather than replace an old door. Although they come from the same family, pine trees used today are faster-growing and softer than those used in the last century. The grain is coarser and the wood weighs less. Old wood has better colour and feels much more solid.

Pine front doors would always have been painted in the past and bare softwood is a very recent fashion. If, however, you decide to strip your door and leave it unpainted, it is important to give the wood several coats of strong weatherproof varnish. Because acrylic varnish is water-based, it is not suitable; marine varnishes, the types used to protect yachts from sea-water damage, are the most durable.

If you have a stained-glass panel that needs repairing, see the information on page 54.

If your original door has not survived (and, sadly, during the housing boom of the late 1970s it was thought best to provide old houses with brand-new doors, most of which are not wearing well), try to find a suitable old replacement. An architectural salvage yard is the best place to look. These yards buy demolition stock, or doors that have come from house conversions. First have a good look around your neighbourhood to see an original door to use as an ideal when searching for your own door. You must also, of course, take accurate measurements of your existing door. You may, like the Walshes, have to settle for one that needs new glass and fittings. If you have no option but to buy a new door, choose one as most like the original as possible.

Front-door furniture

Door-pulls, letterplates, handles, bells, knockers and hinges have served decorative as well as practical purposes since they were first used. Rim locks came into use in the Georgian period, and concealed mortise locks were invented in the late nineteenth century, after which every house was equipped with one. Letterplates and letterboxes only came in after the penny post was introduced in 1840 but were soon fitted to earlier doors, so you are unlikely to come across a door without one unless the letterplate has been placed in the door surround. House numbers also became a standard feature when the postal service was established and were either painted on by signwriters or made of metal and screwed into place.

Builders often saved old fittings that were removed during modernization and demolition work and if yours are missing, look out for replacements in architectural salvage yards or flea markets and junk shops. Reproduction door furniture is available from specialist firms, and the big DIY stores also stock traditional ranges, but do watch the quality, for it may not be as good as the more expensive fittings.

Windows

More aesthetic damage has been done to old buildings by replacement windows than by anything else. Somehow people have been convinced that the most important thing to do is eliminate draughts and that UPVC windows are the way to do it. Unsuspecting home-owners looking around and seeing a lot of this type of window in the neighbourhood tend to think that the product must be good, whereas it is much more likely that the salesforce was good.

Casement windows

Casements were the first type of window that opened. They hinge into the sides of the window frame and open either inwards or outwards. In hot countries where exterior shutters are common, windows are likely to open inwards, so that the two do not conflict. In colder places with high rainfall, the outward opening arrangement works better, and there is less likely to be a need for sun-shading shutters.

Medieval casement windows were set with leaded lights – either in diamond or square patterns of clear glass. During the many revival movements of the nineteenth century, casements came back into fashion from time to time but did not replace the sash window as the most common window until well into the twentieth century.

Sash windows

The first sash windows were introduced in the eighteenth century. These had just one moving sash, which could be propped open using wooden pegs. The weighted double-hung sash was a later development but became the most commonly used window until the 1920s.

The main difference between Georgian and Victorian sash windows is the size of the panes. Early Georgian glass, known as crown glass, was blown and spun, then cut into small panes and arranged in varying numbers of same-sized

squares, depending upon the size of the window. The number of panes ranged from six to twelve in each of the two sashes (i.e. halves) of a window.

During the first half of the nineteenth century cylinder glass became more widely used. It was made by being blown to form a long tube that was split in half, re-heated and then flattened. This meant that one side of the glass was smooth but the other had a slightly puckered surface, which gave a distorted view. Because the glass could be made in bigger sheets, both pane and window sizes increased.

Plate glass, which went into large-scale production in the second half of the nineteenth century, enabled even larger sheets to be made economically for ordinary housing. Sash windows now had single or double panes – one or two in each sash. The increased weight of glass on the frame forced the only major adaptation in sash-window design: 'horns' – the curved wooden supports on the underside of the frame of the top sash – were introduced in about 1850.

Other window styles

Sliding sashes, in which only one of the sashes moves, were first used towards the end of the seventeenth century. One sash can be slid horizontally behind the other and does not need weighting.

Bay windows fell from favour during the years between 1695 and 1851 when the Window Tax was levied, but became very popular once again with the speculatively built suburban developments of the Victorian and Edwardian eras. A bay was an ideal way to break up the frontage of long terraces, while allowing maximum light into the house and providing a good view of the street.

Bow windows, sometimes featuring curved glass set in a curved protruding frame, were popular as shop fronts in Georgian streets and were used later by Regency architects on the upper floors, often with canopies and balconies of wrought iron.

Oriel windows, narrow cantilevered bay windows, sometimes featured in Victorian and Edwardian houses, usually on the first floor to admit light to hallways and stairwells. Always decorative, these were sometimes made with curved or coloured glass in small leaded panes.

Repair, maintenance and replacement of sash windows

Before you condemn any damaged windows, do read *The Repair of Wood Windows*, an excellent pamphlet available from SPAB (see page 186). Replacing old windows should be a very last resort; few are completely beyond repair. A surprising amount of damage can be repaired without removing the window, and future problems can be avoided by regular inspection and redecoration, and by doing your best to prevent condensation forming on the inside by ensuring good ventilation.

Look at all the windows carefully, especially the lower rails where water is likely to sit. If the paint is flaking or peeling, you may find that the wood underneath expands to a spongy texture when wet and is crumbly when dry. Use a pointed instrument like a bradawl to poke the frame in places – if it sinks in, you may have wet rot. To treat wet rot damage, see page 61.

If you strip off clogged layers of paint, take the opportunity to paint the wooden frames with a coat of timber preservative before priming and repainting. Paint sash windows when they are slightly open, then move them to a different position after six hours to prevent them sticking.

If gaps develop between frames and masonry, they should be filled to prevent water getting in. Use mastic (a sealant) applied with a gun, to fill the gaps.

Replacing sash cord

Old sash cords were made of hemp rope that deteriorates over the years. Sash cord today is waxed cotton with a nylon core and it will outlast the house. The cords are concealed in the sides of the window frame behind wooden panels that have to be prised off to reach the rope and weights. Renewing the cord can be tricky, but it is possible to do it yourself by following the instructions opposite. If you do not feel confident about tackling the job, ask friends and neighbours who have sash windows to recommend a local expert who will do the job quickly and cheaply.

Replacing a pane of glass

If your windows have the original glass, a new pane will look obviously different. Old glass has small imperfections that add character to a house, even though they can cause distortion. The closest match that is available is imported

I   Prise off the side beading by sliding a scraper or chisel along the centre to free the paint seal, then move along the length to loosen and remove them both. Pull the lower sash forwards. Now free and remove the parting beading in the same way. Remove the top sash.

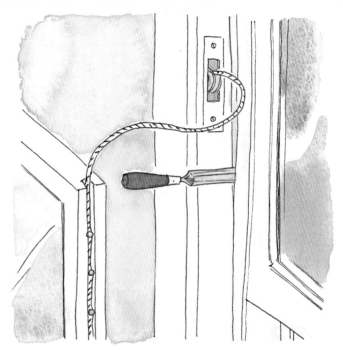

2   Find the removable 'door' that gives access to the sash cord and weights. There may be one for each sash. Remove weight and old cord. Use the old cord as a guide to the length of the new one.

3   Attach a weighted length of string to the end of the new cord and feed it over the pulley, to pull the cord through. Attach the weight to the end of the new cord with a secure knot (see **2**). Nail the other end of the cord into the sash groove of the window using three large-headed nails. Trim any excess and fit the other new cords in the same way. Re-assemble the sash window, using panel pins to secure the beading.

horticultural glass, made for greenhouses. This is actually low-quality glass that has similar characteristics to old glass, like air bubbles and slight ripples.

Wearing thick gloves, chip away all the old glass and putty, and pull out any old sprigs (window-pane tacks). Brush out the rebate. Measure the opening carefully. The replacement glass should be cut 3mm smaller (in both height and width) than the opening, to allow space for the putty.

Roll a lump of putty between your hands to make a rope, then press this into the rebate. Press the glass into the putty, so that the putty squeezes out around the edge. Tap new sprigs around the pane to hold it in place. Press a further rope of putty over these and use a knife to smooth the putty up to the edge

REPLACING QUARRY WORK IN STAINED GLASS

 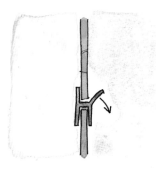 

I   Carefully cut the lead at each corner, using a sharp craft knife.

2   Use the blade to open up the flange and remove the cracked quarry.

3   Replace with the new piece and seal the edges with mastic or a special leaded-light cement. Press the lead flat with a smooth, blunt stick. *

* The cut corners can be re-soldered, but this is not strictly necessary on an internal repair.

of the glazing bar, making a bevel. Putty will smooth easily if you dip the knife in water.

Leave for one month before painting. When you do repaint, overlap the putty slightly with gloss paint to form a weather seal.

Replacing loose putty

Old putty tends to crack and crumble in places; replacing it will prevent water getting in and damaging the woodwork.

Use paint-stripping chemicals to soften areas of hard putty, then scrape it out. Brush out the rebate with a firm brush and replace the putty as described above.

Replacement sash windows

Replacement windows that look exactly the same as the originals are now available. There is no excuse for changing the style; and do not allow anyone to persuade you that UPVC with plastic 'glazing bars' will look like the real thing. A lot of people believe that these new windows are the only way to get a well-insulated, double-glazed unit, but this is no longer true. Traditional-style wooden sash windows are now being made with double glazing, or integral nylon-pile draught excluders.

Companies who provide authentic reproduction wooden sash windows advertise in magazines like BBC *Homes & Interiors*. You may also find a local joiner who is skilled at making sash windows through a local newspaper, or by asking your Conservation Officer for a recommendation.

Decorative Glass

Stained glass

The Victorians loved decorative glass and, in the later part of the period, used it in some form in almost all newly built houses, either in windows, especially for those in halls or landings, or in panels in or around doors. Medieval-style panels with leaded lights were reintroduced by nostalgic movements in architecture in the nineteenth century. The Victorians produced an enormous variety of patterns and colours. Today, because of far less demand, coloured glass is available in far fewer colours, although reclaimed or hand-tinted glass can be found to match and repair broken sections. If you have a damaged stained-glass panel, you can either take it to an expert (look for specialists in restoration magazines, or ask your local glazier to recommend someone) or, if the damage is slight, you could attempt to tackle it yourself – there is great satisfaction in replacing one or two broken pieces.

It is useful to know the technical terms involved, in order to explain the nature of your repair job, or obtain the right materials yourself.

- **Cames** – the lead channels. Either round or flat lead in an H shape.
- **Cement** – mixture of whiting (chalk), linseed oil, turpentine and stove polish. Used between the glass and lead for weatherproofing.
- **Flux** – to help the fusion of lead and solder. Applied before soldering.
- **Jewels** – faceted coloured glass.
- **Quarries** – each glass piece.
- **Roundels** (also known as bull's eyes) – blown glass rounds, still having the concentrated centre where the molten glass was attached for blowing.
- **Solder** – to join leaded pieces together.

Minor repairs

If the glass pieces are rattling about, the old cement may be breaking down. Inspect the window and scrape out any crumbly cement. Use a pointed wooden stick to poke new cement under the lead cames. Leave this to set hard, then polish the glass.

If the panel is buckled (this can happen with age or with pressure), it should be removed and laid flat in a warm place covered with an even weight. It should flatten out in a day or two. If the lead has stretched too much and it will not flatten, the panel may need re-leading; in this case take it to a specialist.

To replace a quarry, follow the step-by-step guide opposite. If you want to put back stained glass that would once have been a feature in your house, either try to find a reclaimed piece of the right age, or commission a new one. You would be lucky to find an old piece that is the right size; smaller panels can be adapted by adding suitable borders; larger ones are not easily adapted. There are many talented stained-glass artists, however, who could make a new panel for you, which would also give you the pleasure of contributing to the design. The Crafts Council (see page 186) will send you a list of people, or you could approach a local art college for the name of a part-time teacher or inspired student.

Etched and sandblasted glass

Acid-etched patterns on sheets of glass were very widely used for bathrooms in terraced houses that were likely to be overlooked. The frosted glass was broken up by repeat patterns of very small motifs that allowed light in without revealing anything to the outside world. A limited selection of patterns is still available. Sandblasting produces much the same effect and was introduced around 1880.

Brilliant-cut and bevelled glass

A star is the most familiar design of the brilliant-cut glass process. It was often cut into deep blue, red or yellow glass panes used as corner pieces in doors and entrance hall windows, and then polished. Bevelled glass has edges cut at an angle and is polished in much the same way to give a bright sparkling effect.

THE WALSHES' FRONT DOOR

When the Walshes took possession of their house the front door was a dismal half-glazed affair, with peeling black paint and a modern reeded glass panel. The only original stained glass left in the house was a fanlight above the door casing. The quest to find the door of their dreams was one of *Home Front*'s most popular features.

The first step was to take very accurate measurements of the existing front door. Then the Walshes set off for the reclamation yard where they eventually found a suitable old door that only needed a couple of millimetres trimmed off to provide a perfect fit. This they stripped and varnished to keep the natural wood look. Unfortunately, the original stained-glass panel was missing, so they decided to have a new one made to their own design.

Armed with a Polaroid camera, the Walshes set off to photograph all the original stained-glass-panelled front doors they could find around the neighbourhood. In the course of their research, they were lucky to find a local glassworks that had been making up stained glass panels since 1888, and were prepared to make a new one for them (P. Eliffs, Mabgate Green, Leeds; tel: 0113 245 2751). There Maxine and Graham were not only able to see the whole process of stained-glass production, but were also able to look through the many pattern books in search of inspiration.

In designing their own panel for the door, they combined elements from the remaining piece of stained glass above their door, the best of their local research, and the pattern they had most liked at the glassworks. A full-sized pattern was drawn up and the colours chosen to harmonize with the existing glass.

The front door was fitted by a local joiner and a sheet of security glass was fixed behind the decorative panel. The total cost of the door, including the 'original' stained-glass panel, was a little over two-thirds of the cost for a brand-new one, and seemed remarkably cheap. The Walshes were delighted with the result. As Maxine said on the programme, 'The door is absolutely gorgeous – it's the door of our dreams. It totally dresses the house from the outside. There's nobody else in Pudsey with a door like ours – so that's quite nice.'

RIGHT *The finished front door with its new stained-glass panel lights up the Walshes' newly decorated entrance hall. The wood panelling below the staircase has been stripped to echo the wood of the door; the original tiled floor has been cleaned, and the walls stencilled.*

INSET *The reclaimed door before the paint was stripped off, propped up in the hallway.*

damp, rot, woodworm and rust

*i*t is probably best to assume that you will find at least one really nasty patch of damp, rot, rust or woodworm in an old house. The chances increase with the age of the property and any length of time that it has stood empty, cold and unventilated. The worst possible scenario involves dry rot, wet rot, cellar fungus and woodworm, but the good thing is that they can all be detected by the same person, a specialist surveyor, and they can all be successfully dealt with. Mortgage companies usually insist on valid timber treatment and damp-proof certificates, both carrying a twenty-year guarantee. So if damp or an infestation has been detected by your mortgage valuation survey, then the company will want a certificate to prove that it has been dealt with. The surveyor's report will recommend

'investigation by an expert' and this is generally taken to mean one of the scores of companies listed in the Yellow Pages, selling chemical damp-proof treatment. The word 'salesman' could often be a substitute for 'expert', so try to find a company that has been in business for quite some time.

Damp

There are three main types of damp. Rising damp comes up through the walls from the ground; penetrating damp comes in through the walls through damaged plaster, brick and pointing; and air-borne moisture inside the house is created when water vapour condenses on cold walls and window panes.

Rising damp usually means either that you do not have a damp-proof course, known as a DPC, or that it has broken down. A DPC is an impermeable layer placed between the foundations and the walls of a house in order to stop water rising up from the soil into the brickwork. The Victorians were the first to discover its merits and since 1870 it has been legally imperative to put one in a new building. Slate, lead or asphalt were used, but these days builders use plastic membranes.

Damp-proofing an old house is done by drilling a lot of holes in a line along the base of the house walls and injecting a chemical solution. The idea is that a reaction takes place within the walls and prevents any more water from rising. Research suggests that it may be more effective just to drill the holes and

ventilate the underfloor area, or, if the chemicals are used, that they should be used under high pressure to saturate the wall, but only when the wall is dry to begin with. None of this is reassuring when your mortgage company would be satisfied just to receive a certificate that the work has been carried out and the company seems happy to issue a guarantee (it is well worth reading the get-out clauses). So what is a house buyer to do?

The advice of the Royal Institute of Chartered Surveyors (RICS, see page 186), is to have a proper survey conducted by a chartered building surveyor. This surveyor's report will be far more detailed and impartial, and more likely to make the distinction between the different types of damp and less likely to recommend treatment that is potentially destructive to the fabric of the house. RICS runs an excellent information desk, and every home should have a copy of their booklet called *Looking After Your Home*.

Air-borne moisture has become a more common problem because houses used to be much better ventilated than they are now. Modern insulation tactics can create damp problems. There are several ways to increase ventilation without simply opening a window: one is to use the fireplace for an open fire. A fire uses up air as it burns, sucking in fresh air as it does so, causing the air to be circulated and replaced. Another way to increase ventilation is to fit self-adhesive strips of brushes to doors and old sash windows; available at DIY stores, these stop draughts without completely sealing off the source of ventilation.

Penetrating damp is dealt with by making repairs to the exterior and allowing the interior walls to dry out gradually. This will only be possible if the interior walls have been coated with a water-permeable paint, i.e. one that allows the walls to breathe. Use a traditional paint, ideally limewash, distemper or a simple emulsion, rather than a waterproof one.

Wet rot

This is the type of rot that affects window frames whose paint has peeled off, leaving them vulnerable to the elements. The wood becomes saturated with water that seeps under the surrounding paint and cannot evaporate through the surface. When the wood does dry out, its fibres collapse, leaving a dry, brittle and crumbly texture behind. If this gets wet again, it swells and absorbs more water and the rot spreads. Further problems develop because these conditions are an ideal breeding ground for fungi – which are living organisms, spread by spores that invade wood and multiply in damp, badly ventilated conditions.

Check for disguised wet rot by poking with

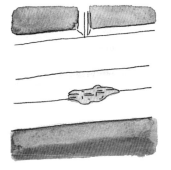

I   Chip away all the rotted wood.

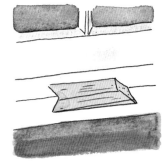

2   Cut into the 'good' wood surrounding the rot, chiselling out a rectangular section. Treat the wood with preservative.

3   Cut a new piece of wood to fit. Treat this with preservative then apply wood glue to all the surfaces and push the piece into place. Clamp till set, then plane level with the surrounding frame. Prime and repaint.

a screwdriver – sound wood will not even be dented but a glossed-over area of rot will dent or be penetrated. All areas of wet rot need dealing with; if the rot is far advanced, all the affected wood must be replaced; if, however, one section of a sill or frame, for example, is damaged, it may be possible to repair it by following our step-by-step guide above.

Dry rot

This is the real enemy – it thrives in damp timber and in areas with bad ventilation and high humidity. It is an indoor and largely invisible fungus that can lurk beneath the wallpaper and paintwork and, once established, can spread destructively throughout a house, attacking the plaster, brickwork and wooden framework. It is a prolific menace.

The fungus first resembles thin, grey strands and then a large fluffy white mass, like cotton wool. Untreated, it mutates into a dense, tangled grey mat that smells strongly of mushrooms. The fruiting bodies are soft and limpet-like with hard white edges and reddish-brown centres. Their presence indicates a well-established colony and they cover an area measured in square metres, emitting millions of spores that look like brick dust.

Treatment for dry rot is radical and must be done professionally. All the affected parts of the house have to be removed and burnt – there is no way to treat it *in situ*. Once the dry rot has been removed, all the surrounding areas have to be thoroughly sterilized with blowlamp flames and a solution of chemicals; and then treated with anti-fungal agents before the repairwork can even begin. This sounds like a home buyer's nightmare but, if detected, it must be faced and dealt with right at the start of your restoration work.

Cellar rot

This affects hard- and softwoods and thrives in damp, cold, stuffy places, like cellars, after which it is named. It is difficult to recognize in the early stages because the surface remains sound, although the wood does change colour, going almost black. Eventually the wood will crumble easily and develop long cracks along the grain. This type of rot can travel across, but will not penetrate, brickwork and the good news is that once the source of the outbreak has been traced, it can be effectively treated and eradicated by eliminating the moisture, applying a fungicide, and then providing some permanent ventilation.

Wood-boring beetles

Four kinds of beetle are prevalent in this country: the common furniture beetle (generally known as woodworm), death-watch beetle, house longhorn beetle and lyctus powder beetle. It is rare to see any of the beetles, but they can be identified by the evidence that they leave behind. They all share the same lifecycle pattern of egg–grub–chrysalis–beetle; then they mate, lay eggs and die off, leaving the next generation to wreak havoc on woodwork. In the natural world these creatures do have a positive purpose to fulfill – they devour dead wood; it is just unfortunate that they cannot differentiate between an uprooted tree and a vital supporting beam or a Chippendale chair.

The wood-boring beetles do their damage during the grub stage, when they can spend as long as four years feasting and excreting, before tunnelling towards the surface and making a hole where they assume their chrysalis state. Once they emerge as mature beetles, they bore to the surface and exit, leaving recognizably distinctive-sized holes and dust residues.

Common furniture beetle

Common by name and common by nature, this beetle attacks every kind of wood from the finest seasoned hardwood to new plywood and, as a result, is the one most likely to be found in the average house. It is about 4mm

long and emerges between June and August. The holes the beetles leave are 2mm round and the dust surrounding the holes is coarse, sandy and cigar-shaped.

Death-watch beetle

This creature is unlikely to be found anywhere but in properties that are over 200 years old. It needs a degree of moisture in order to thrive, but generally attacks only very well-seasoned hardwoods, and has a preference for oak, chestnut and elm. The beetles' most distinctive feature is their mating signal, which is made by both males and females banging their heads against the woodwork.

The beetles are quite large – between 7mm and 9mm long – and they leave 3mm round exit-holes when they emerge between March and June, leaving coarse, bun-shaped pellets.

House longhorn beetle

This is a Continental import that infests the sapwood (the outer layer, just beneath the bark) of seasoned softwood used in roof timbers. It is the largest of the wood-boring beetles, measuring between 10mm and 25mm, and it leaves 5mm x 8mm oval holes. Its size reflects its appetite and destructive potential. Check for the large exit-holes between June and September and look for soft, floury cylinders of bore-dust.

Lyctus powder beetle

This beetle eats only hardwoods and likes them quite fresh – about twenty years old, so you are unlikely to encounter it in an old house unless some timber has been replaced fairly recently. The beetles thrive in timber yards, so it is worth knowing what to look out for if you are buying new timber. The damage that they inflict can be distinguished from that of other beetles because it occurs in layers rather than tunnels. They are 5mm long and leave 2mm round exit-holes when they emerge between May and September. Their bore-dust is a fine, soft powder.

Treatment for an infestation

Treatments either involve saturating the wood with the correct chemical solution or fumigation. If the infestation is small, then – with the exception of death-watch beetle which must be dealt with by experts – you will be able to treat it with the appropriate solution yourself. Ask a builder's merchant for advice. Fumigation and large-scale treatment with chemicals are professional jobs. Try to choose a specialist company with a good reputation. This type of work tends to be franchised, so it is advisable to find somebody who has been doing it for several years. You do not want a beginner in charge of noxious chemicals.

Rust

If your home has decorative iron railings on a balcony or at street level, you should consider

yourself lucky – much of this type of decoration was recycled to help the war effort as the result of an appeal in 1941.

If you have railings or fittings that are affected by surface rust, it can be removed either by wire brushing or professional sandblasting. The stripped surface should be treated with a rust inhibitor before repainting. Use a good primer and special metal paint.

If the ironwork needs mending or parts are missing, you will need a specialist firm to carry

ABOVE *Basement rooms need not be dank, dark and musty, as the freshness of this dining room proves. Ensure that there is good ventilation and treat walls with water-permeable paint such as limewash or distemper. If a flagstone floor is damp, it may need to be relaid with a new damp-proof course.*

out the repairs and replacements. You can find one by contacting The Guild of Architectural Ironmongers (see page 186).

woodwork and
decorative plasterwork

five

oodwork and decorative plasterwork were important features in all Georgian, Victorian and Edwardian houses. Both were quick to reflect the changes in fashion, and so are good clues to dating your house. Whatever original period details you inherit are worth preserving and, once restored, they provide the perfect framework for the colour and pattern that you choose for your walls, floors, fabrics and furniture.

Internal doors

Original doors are a real asset in any period home; they will follow the proportions of the house and the decorative style of the period. Throughout the Georgian, Victorian and Edwardian eras internal doors were usually panelled, sometimes glazed and, unless made from hardwoods, they would have been painted. The panels were lined with decorative mouldings, or raised and fielded with a bevelled edge, adding a sense of depth. Georgian doors in the grander houses would have been made from highly polished hardwoods, finely crafted with two or more panels. The Victorians also used hardwood where they could afford it. Softwood doors were often treated to look like hardwood using woodgraining techniques, or sometimes marbled or stencilled. They were also draped with heavy curtains and pelmets called portières.

The arrangement of the panels changed in Edwardian houses, so that the longest were in the bottom two-thirds of the doors with shorter ones above. Doors were either of light, natural wood, preferably oak, or painted white or cream with Arts and Crafts or Art Nouveau-style door furniture.

What are now known as double reception rooms were originally divided by folding doors that could be opened up to make one large

PREVIOUS PAGES *The gleaming floorboards, solid panelled doors, fine wooden mouldings and plasterwork all contribute to the elegance of this beautiful old house.*

RIGHT *Original or reclaimed double doors like these can give the best of both worlds: a large open space, but one that can be divided. The stripped-pine Victorian doors have their original glazing bars but although the new glass is the appropriate colour, the square corner-panes might well originally have had 'brilliant-cut' stars. The window at the far end of the room has space for shutters that have sadly been lost.*

room for parties. Unfortunately many were lost during the craze for open-plan rooms, when internal walls were removed and dining rooms went out of fashion. As the reinstatement of a big feature like this would make such a difference to the way you use your reception rooms, it is certainly worth looking into architectural salvage yards, or asking a couple of carpenters to measure up and give you an estimate on the price of making a set of replacement folding doors. Dividing a room like this can save on heating bills and also provide a separate dining room or workspace.

As glass manufacture developed (see page 51), so glazed panels began to be used in doors to admit more natural light through adjoining rooms. Glazed double doors were a particular feature of Victorian hallways. The glazed panels were sometimes etched with patterns, or framed with stained glass held in wooden glazing bars. If you have glazed internal doors with damaged stained glass or missing brilliant-cut corner-panes, it is possible to buy replacements, both new and old.

A great number of panelled doors were covered with sheets of hardboard during the 1950s and 1960s when plain flush doors became fashionable. If you have an old house with flush doors, take a close look, and scrape back the paintwork along one inside face to see whether you have the real thing.

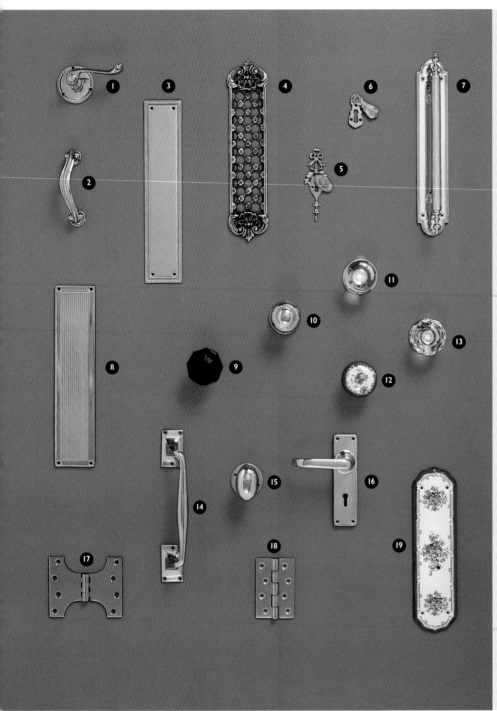

Reproduction Interior Door Furniture

1 **Lever handle** (Georgian)
2 **Balmoral pull handle** (Victorian)
3 **Fingerplate** (Georgian)
4 **Ornate brass finger-plate** (Georgian)
5 **Bow escutcheon** (Regency/Victorian)
6 **Ornate escutcheon** (Late Georgian/ Victorian)
7 **Princess pull handle** (Queen Anne Revival)
8 **Reeded doorplate** (Regency)
9 **Black cast-iron door knob** (Victorian)
10 **Mortice knob** (Georgian)
11 **Acrylic 'glass' mortice knob** (Edwardian)
12 **Floral mortice knob** (Victorian)
13 **Faceted acrylic 'cut glass' mortice knob** (Edwardian)
14 **Brass pull handle** (Victorian/Edwardian)
15 **Oval brass mortice knob** (Edwardian)
16 **Lever lock** (Victorian/Edwardian)
17 **Parliament hinge** (Victorian)
18 **Brass and steel butt hinges** (Victorian/ Edwardian)
19 **Porcelain fingerplate** (Victorian/Edwardian)

Consider stripping off the old paint, even if you do intend to repaint the doors, because the edges, panels and mouldings will all look a lot sharper once the old paint layers have been removed. (See the paint-stripping section on page 75.) Holes can be filled with wood filler, or a mixture of sawdust and wood glue, then sanded level once dry. Cracks in the panels often occur when they have been glued in place, instead of left loose to cope with the expansion or contraction that happens with changes in the atmosphere and temperature. Free the panels, if possible, and apply wood glue to the edges of the crack, then tape it closed with masking tape while the glue dries. Mouldings can be re-pinned, but do use a nail punch to punch the nail heads below the surface of the wood and then fill the holes.

Wooden doors should not be left bare, and even if you are keeping the wood natural, you should treat it with a nourishing coat of Danish oil (a mixture of alkyd resins and natural oils) and then polish the wood with an antiquing beeswax, which not only gives a subtle sheen but also has a most delicious smell.

If you are repainting doors, start with a primer, then use an undercoat and a topcoat. Flat colour is generally more suitable for a period house than gloss.

Internal door furniture

Just as their plain brass door handles reflected the Georgians' love of simplicity, the Victorians' taste for ornate decoration resulted in door handles, escutcheons (keyhole covers) and fingerplates in a multitude of styles, in materials such as china, bronze, glass and enamelware. The more substantial designs were used in the reception rooms and more delicate gilded or floral sets featured on the upper floors. The Victorians became rather obsessed with

hygiene after several devastating epidemics of typhoid and cholera, and wipeable fingerplates were sometimes put below as well as above the door handles, so that both adult and children's germs could be easily wiped away.

Restoring old door furniture

If you inherit door furniture caked in layers of paint or tarnished by life in the open air, you can enjoy the rewarding job of returning it to its former glory. Paint can be stripped with chemicals. (Always wear protective rubber gloves when using paint stripper, or strong chemicals of any kind.) Place the bits in a foil dish and saturate their surfaces with the stripper. Leave until the paint has softened, then use wire wool to rub it off. Caustic soda can also be used. Make up a strong solution in a glass or china dish and soak the door furniture in it. Take great care with caustic soda – it gives off fumes and will burn the skin. Take particular care when immersing the fittings; always wear rubber gloves and protect your eyes from splashes. Wash away the caustic solution in an outside drain, scrubbing away the softened paint with a plastic brush, and rinse the fittings in clean water. Although it sounds drastic, it is a very efficient method of removing old paint.

Stripped iron should be treated with a rust inhibitor, then primed and painted black. Tarnished brass can be cleaned with a tablespoon each of salt and vinegar mixed in a cup of hot water. Rub this into the surface using fine wire wool, then dry and buff to a shine.

Shutters

Along with internal room-dividing doors, internal window shutters were also one of the casualties of the 1950s and 1960s. Many Georgian and early Victorian houses had folding panelled shutters that hinged back into a recess in the wall beside the windows, known as a shutter box. Shutters always covered the lower half of the window; fashion dictated whether the rest was covered. They had, and still have, many advantages: they give increased security and insulation, and do away with the need for expensive curtaining. If you find empty shutter boxes in your house, and want to reinstate wooden shutters, they can easily be made and fitted by any qualified joiner. You will need to use old pine if you want to leave them unpainted; a cheaper option is to use MDF (medium density fibreboard) and paint it.

Rolling shutters, which were housed in a box below the window and could be pulled up to be hooked over the window, were more often left in place when they went out of fashion. If you have a Victorian house with an unusually broad wooden panel below the window, look along the edges of the sill – there may be hinges that allow it to be flapped back to reveal long-lost rolling shutters.

Decorative woodwork

Wood was used for decorative mouldings and cornices long before plaster came into use in the late seventeenth century. Skirting, dado rails, picture rails and cornices were originally parts of a fully wood-panelled wall. As smooth plaster began to become more fashionable, the amount of wood used gradually decreased. By the mid-eighteenth century only the area between the dado rail and skirting board, known as the wainscot, was still sometimes panelled, while picture rails marked the lower extent of the frieze at the top of the wall. The architraving around doors was wide and classically styled. Wood mouldings became simpler still during the Regency: the dado rail disappeared, leaving only a picture rail, simple skirting board and fluted architrave.

The Victorian era saw a return to heavier-style wooden mouldings. The Gothic Revival brought back the dado rail and even carved wood panelling in grander houses, skirting boards grew to over 30cm high and featured complicated mouldings, and architraves around doors and windows became wider.

The influence of the Arts and Crafts movement can be seen in the woodwork of a number of houses built around the turn of the century. Natural wood, particularly light-coloured oak, became popular for fitted cupboards, fireplaces, surrounds, architraves and floorboards. If you live in a house of this period it is worth stripping paint from inconspicuous woodwork to see whether it is oak that could be returned to its original state. Wood panelling, including matchboarding, was often used in entrance halls, so it could be worth investigating behind the wallpaper.

At this time, built-in furniture became more common, with cupboards upstairs, glass-fronted display cabinets in the dining room and a display shelf at picture-rail height to show off plates and ornaments. Kitchens had built-in dressers and wooden overmantels adorned fireplaces.

Replacing and restoring woodwork

If you have to replace just a section of wood moulding, make a pattern using a profile gauge and make a full-sized drawing of the existing moulding. It is worth visiting a timber merchant to look through samples and catalogues to see if there is a moulding that matches yours. If not, any good carpenter will be able to make up a new piece. If you have only a small part of an original moulding left, it would be far cheaper to replace it all with new off-the-shelf moulding of the same style and proportions. All softwood

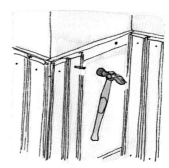

1   Using a tape measure, straight-edge and spirit level, mark the positions of the top, lower and middle strips of batten that will support the matchboarding. Insert wallplugs and screw the battens in place.

2   Place the first board in a corner and check that it is vertical. You may find that the walls are a bit wonky: if so trim the edge of this first board at the wall edge, so that all the subsequent ones fit vertically.

3   Fit the tongues of the boards into the grooves, but use a piece of scrap timber to protect the edge as you hammer them together. Tap down from the top to keep the line straight.

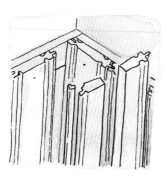

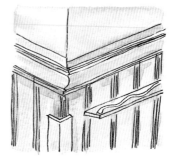

4   The final board may need cutting down to fit the space. Make a paper template the size of the gap; draw a cutting line on the board and saw off the waste. If the board is the right size, simply strip off the tongue before fitting it.

5   Neaten off the top by fitting a dado rail moulding, and the base with skirting. Measure it to fit and mitre the ends. Use either nails or countersunk screws to fix, then fill the holes with wood filler.

6   Use strips of thin, plain beading to fill the gaps between dado rail and wall; glue and pin them in place. Cover the corners of the matchboarding with thin corner-beading, glued and pinned in place.

would originally have been painted, so if you are after authenticity, forget stripped pine.

Matchboarding, also known as tongue-and-groove, is an easy way to add wood panelling to walls. It was commonly used throughout the Victorian and Edwardian eras, and is a treatment that suits hallways, bathrooms, kitchens and small bedrooms, particularly in small unpretentious houses. Matchboarding kits, with all the timber cut to the same height, can be bought from DIY stores, or you can follow the step-by-step guide above.

Stripping wood

Although there is no historical precedent for stripped pine, it is deservedly popular and can look good in a period setting. Old pine has a warm glow when polished and the effect is very comfortable and homely – it is also true that it does away with the problem of worn and chipped paintwork. Also, by stripping pine you are not interfering with the fabric of the house – the wood can always be painted at some future date, and in the meantime it will have benefited from the removal of layers of old paint.

Doors, shutters, panelling and other flat surfaces can be stripped using scrapers and a hot-air gun – which is like a very hot hair drier. The heat causes the paint to bubble up; it should be scraped off while still warm and soft. Aim for the corners or any raised or recessed detailing first. Chemical strippers are far more messy but, provided you follow the manufacturer's instructions, and take precautions to protect your skin and the surrounding area, they can be used to strip paint and are the only option for more complex surfaces such as architraves. As most chemical strippers generally penetrate only two layers of paint at one time, several applications may be necessary.

The other option for removable woodwork, such as doors, is to have them dipped in a caustic tank. There are hot tanks, which do the job very quickly, and cold tanks that take longer, so are more expensive, but are gentler on the wood. The problem with caustic solutions is that they raise the grain of the wood; and they are indiscriminate and can eat away the glue which binds the door together. Once the wood has dried out, it will need sanding and its natural oils will need replenishing with one or two coats of Danish oil. Check the joints and re-glue them if necessary.

Decorative plasterwork

Plaster is a versatile material that has been used both for decoration and for plain wall and ceiling surfaces for at least 500 years. Huge deposits of gypsum were discovered under Montmartre in the thirteenth century – this is where the name plaster of Paris comes from. Plaster is made with either gypsum and slaked lime or gypsum mixed with sand and water. Other ingredients, particularly hair, were added to bind it together. Recipes for stucco plaster include ground marble dust, lard, curdled milk and egg white, all of which were added to give it more strength or elasticity.

As the Georgian vogue for intricate plasterwork spread, new inventions made it possible for plaster ornament to be cast quite cheaply and soon all houses had decorative plaster features. Robert Adam and his brother made a huge impact with their patent 'compo' – plaster-based material that was pressed into reverse-carved boxwood moulds to make very fine mouldings. Swags, urns, columns and medallions appeared on fireplaces, friezes and wall panels. Ceilings were decorated with circles of fine moulded ribbons and swags, joined by urns and classical figures.

The Victorians' love of opulence and elaborate decoration pushed the plaster-moulding process along and the invention of fibrous plaster, which was strengthened on a layer of strong canvas, made bigger and fancier mouldings possible. In the early part of the period a fashion for Tudor-style decoration brought naturalistic floral and animal patterns arranged in heavy panels on the ceilings. Later, large ornamental ceiling roses developed in response to the arrival of piped gas and the use of central gaslights. The ceiling roses were used to disguise the pipes and provide ventilation through a series of holes in the moulded

Reproduction Plasterwork Mouldings

1. **Egg and dart cornice** *(Georgian)*
2. **Adam ceiling rose** *(Late Georgian)*
3. **Ceiling rose** *(Victorian)*
4. **Flower frieze** *(Victorian)*
5. **Cherub corbel** *(Victorian)*
6. **Lady's head corbel** *(Late Victorian)*
7. **Roman vine panel moulding** *(Late Victorian/ Edwardian)*
8. **Ceiling rose** *(Victorian)*

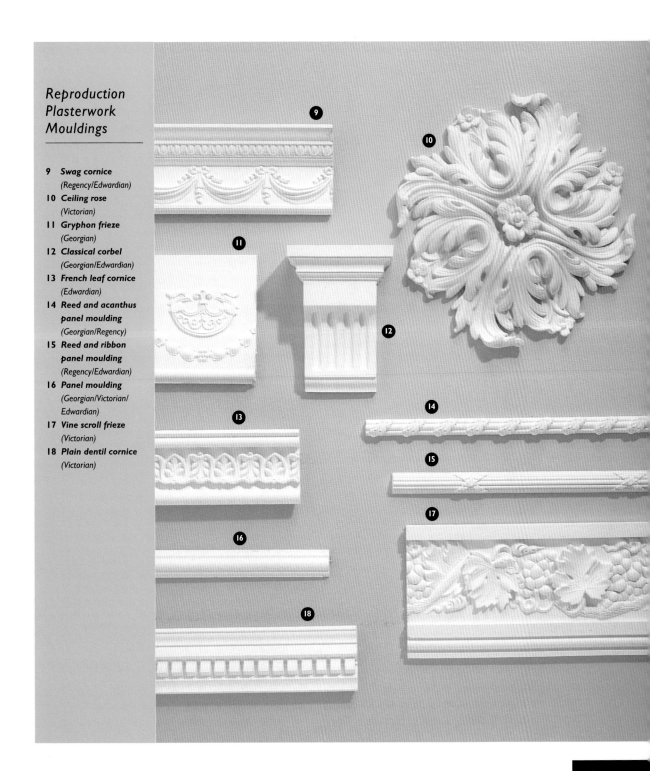

Reproduction Plasterwork Mouldings

9 **Swag cornice**
   (Regency/Edwardian)
10 **Ceiling rose**
   (Victorian)
11 **Gryphon frieze**
   (Georgian)
12 **Classical corbel**
   (Georgian/Edwardian)
13 **French leaf cornice**
   (Edwardian)
14 **Reed and acanthus panel moulding**
   (Georgian/Regency)
15 **Reed and ribbon panel moulding**
   (Regency/Edwardian)
16 **Panel moulding**
   (Georgian/Victorian/ Edwardian)
17 **Vine scroll frieze**
   (Victorian)
18 **Plain dentil cornice**
   (Victorian)

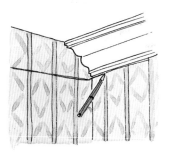

1   Using a piece of cornice as a guide, draw a line along the wall to mark its position. Cut along this line with a craft knife.

2   Peel the wallpaper off to the bare plaster down to this line.

3   Scratch up the surface of the plaster to provide a good 'key' for the adhesive.

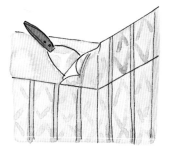

4   Make a paper pattern by smoothing thin paper over the cornice then marking the mitre at 45°; or place the cornice in a mitre box. (Do not cut the strip to the correct length yet, in case you need to adjust the mitres to fit.)

5   Saw through the cornice, either in a mitre box or freehand with a pattern guide. Check that the two ends fit comfortably – slight imperfections can be put right with filler. Cut the other ends in the same way.

6   Use adhesive that is recommended by the manufacturers of the cornice, and mix according to their instructions. Spread this along the cornice on the edges that will meet the ceiling and the wall.

decoration. The weight of the ceiling roses was echoed by increasingly heavy, ornate cornices. By the Edwardian era things had become a lot plainer and a mixture of styles was popular, including Adam-style ribbons and swags, and the swirling patterns of Art Nouveau. The heavy patterns and shapes were considered old-fashioned and the whole effect became lighter and less dominating.

Surface decoration was so integral a part of nineteenth-century interiors that materials which could imitate plasterwork were soon developed and manufactured. Papier mâché began being used around 1850 and could be

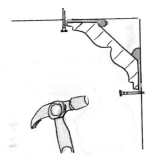

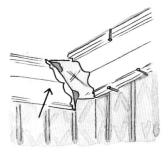

7   Press the cornice firmly in to the wall and up to the ceiling; tap in some nails to support it while the adhesive bonds. (The holes can be filled once the nails have been removed.)

8   Treat the adjoining cornice in the same way, applying adhesive along the mitred edge as well. Press closely together where they meet and add supporting nails to hold this section as well. Fill any gaps with adhesive or filler.

9   Use a stiff bristled brush to clean any excess adhesive from the edges before it dries.

cast in the same type of mould to produce a much lighter material that could give even sharper detailing, and this was painted white to look like the real thing. Another development, in 1877, was the invention of Lincrusta, a thick moulded wall covering with a raised pattern that looked like plaster relief-work. (It is now available from specialist supplier.) We are more familiar with anaglypta, the papier mâché version, which followed ten years later and was cheaper to produce and easier to apply. This type of finish was often used below the dado rail, especially in halls and stairways, to gave extra protection to the wall; and sometimes as a frieze above the picture rail. It is notoriously hard to remove and became one of the most loathed wall coverings for many years when people were trying to modernize old houses. If you do have old anaglypta it is best to learn to love it, because one of the reasons for its popularity was its ability to hide a multitude of sins – it may be holding your wall together.

Restoring plaster decoration

If you have a moulding or ceiling rose that looks as if it has been clogged up with many layers of paint, you will probably be amazed by the sharpness of the details once it has been cleaned. It is very likely that chalky distemper has been used: this can be removed by dampening the paint with a water sprayer and using a sharp tool to scrape and chip it off carefully. If it is covered in a vinyl-based paint, a chemical stripper will be needed; this must be washed off before repainting. Both processes are very time-consuming, so if you want a painter/decorator to do the work, get a firm quote for the job rather than employing someone on an hourly rate.

If you have damaged cornices, they can usually be repaired *in situ*. Although cornices are now made in a workshop and then stuck in place, rather than being made on the spot using 'running moulds', most good plasterers, especially those with some experience or an interest in conservation, will be able to run a mould and could repair or replace one. Ask your Conservation Officer or your builder if they can recommend someone locally. You can also buy sections of decorative plaster mouldings from specialists and the larger DIY chains – and if the pattern used in your house was a popular one, you will probably still be able to match it.

Replacing plasterwork

If the cornice, ceiling rose or plaster mouldings have been removed, it would be cheaper to buy off-the-shelf replacement sections. Look at similar houses in your neighbourhood to gain an idea of the style that would suit your house. Remember that proportion is all-important; a moulding that looks relatively large in the store may look small and mean around a high ceiling in a large room. Take a sample section home and try it before making a commitment. There are also some very fancy wooden mouldings that can be used to replace plaster cornicing. These can be painted to look like plaster and

are easier to handle, cut and fix in position than the plaster variety. There are even polystyrene versions of cornices and roses that, once painted, look like plaster. However, as this material has not stood the test of time, it would probably be better to stick to plaster or wood.

If you have one good plaster bracket but others are damaged or missing, it is possible to make a mould from which to cast your own replacements. Mould-making kits are available from craft and hobby suppliers and the process is not difficult to manage. First clean the paint from the original, so that the new ones are as sharp-edged as possible. Coat the original with the mixture, according to the manufacturer's instructions, and once it has set, peel off the mould and use it to recast the shape in plaster. Attach it to the wall by first coating the back of the moulding and the wall with PVA glue and allowing it to dry. This will give an even surface for the bonding agent and stop the plaster from absorbing it. Thereafter follow the instructions for putting up a cornice on page 78.

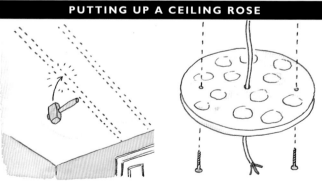

PUTTING UP A CEILING ROSE

1 Locate the central ceiling joists by tapping gently with a mallet. The ceiling rose needs to be fixed into two joists, so measure out and drill holes for four brass screws.

2 Thread the light flex through the centre of the rose. Apply dabs of fixing plaster or plasterboard joint-filler to the rose then press it into position. Secure with the brass screws.

RIGHT *A beautifully preserved example of Art Nouveau Lincrusta, below the dado, still decorates the hallway. There is a low-relief plaster frieze in the room on the left.*

fireplaces

When central heating became widespread, a fairly recent phenomenon in Great Britain, many fireplaces were removed, bricked up or simply covered over to give an old house a more 'modern' feel. Eventually, though, people began to realize that something was missing. A fireplace was so much more than a heat source: it was a focal point; a decorative feature; a useful shelf for ornaments and an all-round ice-breaker. An open fire is a creature comfort.

The decorative possibilities inherent in fireplaces were not generally exploited until the eighteenth century. Designers like Inigo Jones spearheaded the Classical Revival and built massive 'temple style' fireplaces, complete with sculptured statuary, pediments and columns. Robert Adam's interpretation of the classical style was lighter and his fireplace designs more in scale with their surroundings. His designs continue to be popular right up to the present day. Not all eighteenth-century fireplaces were elaborate; some were simple and elegant with moulded stone, marble or wooden surrounds set into wood-panelled walls.

The older-style fireplaces were designed for log burning and used dog grates – four-legged baskets that stood in the fire opening. These were unsuitable for coal, as were the wide chimneys. The coal burned incompletely and too fast so that the air became filled with particles of soot. The first person to attempt to find a solution to the problem of air pollution caused by coal fires was an American, Count Rumford. He had a passion for the subject and set about studying every aspect of fireplaces and chimney design. Eventually, in 1799, he published his findings. As a result of these the register grate was invented. This is the type that is so familiar – a cast-iron, splay-fronted fixture that fits into the fire opening in a chimney breast with an integral fire-back and grate. The Victorians loved inventions and soon took out patents on all sorts of adaptations that would make fires burn better and use less fuel.

The Victorians were also the first to see fireplaces as pieces of furniture. They designed fireplaces to go with all the revivalist styles – Tudor, Gothic, Georgian and Queen Anne – and wherever there was an opportunity for decoration they used it. Factories mass-produced cast-iron surrounds, ceramic tiles, fancy mirrored overmantels and a wealth of brass accessories to match. When marble was beyond their budgets, the Victorians imitated it using slate, painting on the veins in the same way as they painted pine to look like mahogany. They introduced the mantel drape – often made of velvet brocade with a trimmed edge of baubles or tassels. Some even went so far as to change the fire surrounds when they redecorated. Bedroom fireplaces were far more restrained than those downstairs, and those in servants' rooms were tiny – just big enough for a few coals from the kitchen range at bedtime.

At the end of the nineteenth century, the Arts and Crafts movement reintroduced the inglenook – an old country fireplace that took up the whole chimney breast and had seating on either side of the fire. Although the ideals of the movement focused on the dignity of the craftsman and the honesty of simple country design, the houses that reflected their principles must have cost a fortune to build. As far as the mass-production market was concerned, Art

Nouveau was a more popular decorative style. Edwardian houses were often fitted with wooden overmantels, brass and copper fire-hoods and fancy tiled borders. There was also another classical revival at the beginning of this century when grand fireplaces were supported on columns, though they stopped short of mantel statues.

Restoring an old fireplace

If you have inherited an old fireplace that needs attention and saw *Home Front*'s feature on the Walshes' restoration of their fireplaces, you will know just how rewarding the effort can be.

Rusty cast iron can be cleaned up with a rust-removing solution after loose particles have been removed with a wire brush. Rust damage is usually confined to the surface and, once it has been dealt with, should be treated immediately with a coat of rust inhibitor. Cracks in the firebrick can be repaired with fire cement.

If the fireplace surround has been painted, you will want to strip it. First carefully scrape off a small area to discover the material beneath the paint. Wood surrounds can either be taken off and stripped in a caustic tank, or can be stripped *in situ* with either a hot-air gun or a chemical paint stripper. (If you use paint stripper, tape your sleeves to long rubber gloves to avoid any possibility of splashing unprotected skin.) Metal-work is best cleaned by sandblasting or using a chemical stripper, and finished with the metal burnishing attachment on an electric drill. Once stripped, cast iron should not be painted. Grates used to be blackened with black lead polish. Similar products, containing graphite to avoid the dangers of lead poisoning, are available today. Rub grate polish into all the ironwork, then buff it up with a soft duster.

If your fireplace has fine raised detailing – Adam-style for instance – this may be made of gesso. If so, go carefully with a non-water-based chemical stripper, as it would not survive extreme heat, or being soaked with water.

Marble can be cleaned with special products but first try giving it a good scrub with a bristle brush and clean warm water. If the grime is ingrained, invest in some Bell's Special Marble Cleaner No. 7, which can be obtained through mail order (see page 186). This product can be used in different dilutions, the strongest of all being a stiff poultice mixture that is left in place for three days to draw the impurities out of the marble. The same company also makes cleaning products for slate, stone and ceramic tiles, but in all cases their advice is to try sponging and scrubbing with clean warm water first.

Ceramic tiles in the fireplace surround are best cleaned with warm water, washing-up liquid and a soft cloth. Never wipe tiles when they are hot because it may cause crazing of the glaze. If the tiles are scorched, try a non-abrasive household cleaner on a cloth. Repeated rubbing with gentle pressure is better than scratching or scraping, which could damage the glazed surface. The tiles can only be replaced from the back, which necessitates removing the whole installation from the wall.

Stone can be scrubbed with a detergent solution but not soap, which can be absorbed and cause discoloration. A very grimy stone fireplace can be scrubbed with a weak solution of household bleach, then rinsed with clean water and dried.

Slate can be made to glow again by applying white wax polish and buffing with a soft duster.

Before you use any product, check that it is suitable for surfaces near a heat source.

If you decide to open up or restore an old fireplace, have it checked by a chimney sweep. Choose one who is a member of the National Association of Chimney Sweeps (NACS, see page 186), because they work to regulated standards. It is important that the chimney is not obstructed and that the smoke cannot leak out into the house. If a fire is to work efficiently it must be connected to a sound chimney and the correct-sized flue. If the lining of the chimney is in poor condition it may need re-lining. There are several ways of doing this, including inserting rigid or flexible metal liners; pumping concrete around a rubber tube that is removed after the concrete has hardened; or spraying on concrete with a device that revolves within the chimney.

The choice of liner depends to some extent on your choice of fuel. There are flue liners made especially for open fire-effect gas fires, and while all liners that suit solid fuel will also be fine for gas, it does not work the other way round.

All of this work – the diagnosis, selection of the lining method and the installation – must be done by a specialist.

Replacing a fireplace

If you have a chimney breast but no fireplace, check behind the wallpaper before investing in a whole fireplace. Often mantelpieces were removed but the fireplace itself was left intact. Equally, fireplaces were removed to make way for modern electric or gas fires, leaving the mantelpiece in position. If so, you can tile the inside of the opening with heat-resistant tiles and fireproof cement, and then use a fire basket to hold the fuel – a cheaper alternative to a complete period fireplace.

If you decide to put back a fireplace that is in keeping with the style and date of your house, begin by asking to see your neighbours' original fireplaces if they are still in place, or seek the advice of a dealer who specializes in restoring old fireplaces. Apart from appropriate style, the other important factor to bear in mind when choosing a new fireplace is proportion: it should neither overwhelm the room, nor look mean. Because Victorian bedroom fireplaces tend to be smaller and less elaborate than ones orginally made for reception rooms, they are often chosen for living rooms today.

If you know nothing about the working aspects of a fireplace it is well worth buying through a specialist, because they will have repaired or replaced any broken parts, and usually provide a fitting service as well. Reproduction fireplaces that are made to exactly the same patterns as the originals are also available, and with these you have the advantage of being supplied with all the necessary parts. You can have them installed to meet Building Regulations standards and will also get some form of guarantee.

If you do find a wonderful old cast-iron fireplace, don't buy it until you have satisfied all the points on the following list:

- Check that it will fit the fire opening in your chimney breast. Take accurate measurements of the chimney breast and the opening and mark them on a diagram.
- Check for any cracks in the fire-back.
- Check that the lugs for the screws that will hold the fireplace to the wall are there, and unbroken.
- Check to see whether the plaster that holds the tiles is new – this could mean the tiles are reproduction rather than original.
- Check all the pieces are there – especially the grate bars, back section and ash can.

Woodburning and solid fuel stoves

These stoves, first invented in Sweden in 1747, have never gone out of fashion in Northern Europe, where their efficiency has long been

German Folk Art

appreciated. There is now an expanding market in Britain and there is a tremendous variety to choose from, especially in 'nostalgic' designs. Some use coal, others wood; some can be connected to a back boiler to heat radiators and provide hot water. Most are cast iron, although some decorative ceramic types are also available and, if you want a more up-to-date feel without losing the essential shape of an old stove, look at some of the enamelled stoves, which come in a good range of colours. Many cast-iron stoves are still made from the original nineteenth-century patterns and look perfect in old houses, but they do need a Grade 1 flue.

Stoves offer the best of both worlds: you can have the security of an enclosed fire that is easy to keep clean, and you can open up the doors whenever you like to have the added comfort of an open fire.

The gas fire option

Gas-fuelled coal-effect fires have come a long way since they were first introduced. The originals looked impressive, but were unconvincing because of their low heat output and coals that looked too good to be true. The mechanisms have now become so sophisticated that you can light up by remote control, vary the flame to flicker or glow, and vary the warmth output through a convector box. You can also have a gas fire fitted regardless of whether a chimney exists or not.

Gas fires can be installed in existing old fireplaces or bought as a complete unit in any period style. Among the most genuine-looking are the stoves. They come in all shapes and sizes, and with the glass doors shut and the flames blazing away it is impossible to tell that the coals are actually ceramic. They are tremendously heat-efficient, they can be fitted into an ordinary fireplace chimney and the big bonus is that there is no mess.

All gas appliances must be installed by a professional CORGI (Council for Registered Gas Installers) registered fitter (see page 186).

Fireplace accessories

Once your fireplace is restored or installed, there is a wealth of useful and decorative accessories to choose from. If you have a tiled hearth, a brass fender is the traditional surround, and can be bought from antique shops or as a reproduction. Though many different styles and sizes exist, it may be easier to tile a hearth to fit a fender than find a fender of the right size, particularly if you want an old one. Old brass has a better colour than new, and any slight dents in the surface seem to suit the material. Building Regulations demand that new fireplaces have raised hearths, and a lovely brass fender is a good way to mark the boundary with the rest of the floor.

Sets of fire implements including a shovel, brush, poker and tongs are essential if you have a coal fire, and will strengthen the illusion if you opt for gas. An attractive coal scuttle or log basket can make all the difference when the fire needs fuel on a cold winter's night. Beware of overdoing things, however. Don't dress up an already decorative fireplace with fire dogs, lots of implements, a gleaming brass fender and an ornamental coal scuttle. The fire itself should always be the star.

THE WALSHES' FIREPLACE

coal had once burned. This was removed by a qualified gas fitter, and the chimney was checked, swept and pronounced safe.

Local fireplace restorer, Phil Lynas, then came in to help. Beneath the many layers of paint, the surround was found to be of slate and ceramic tiles. The slate was stripped using Nitromors and scrapers. (Anyone who saw the feature will have noticed that Phil did this with his bare hands – don't try this at home. Always wear rubber gloves and goggles when using this caustic substance.) The final flecks of paint were removed using wire wool soaked in white spirit. Phil advised using a more gentle treatment for the tiles; though the same chemical was applied, wire wool was used instead of scrapers.

An electric burnisher was used to polish up the cast-iron details. Then Zebrite, a graphite polish, was applied and, when dry, brushed clean of the surface powder and buffed up.

Interior designer Peter Plaskitt showed Maxine how to finish off the incised pattern in the slate by gilding it with real gold leaf (available at craft shops). You can follow her example by using the step-by-step guide below.

The Walshes were extremely lucky to find every original fireplace still in place in their house. The front-room fireplace was covered in paint, and an old gas fire had been fitted where

ADDING GILDING TO A FIRE SURROUND

1   Ensure the slate is clean and totally grease-free. Using a fine artist's paintbrush paint gold size into the pattern.

2   Using the end of a paintbrush or a fingernail, gently smooth the gold leaf in place on the pattern.

3   Brush away all the excess gold leaf with a stiff bristled brush. Burnish with a soft cloth.

RIGHT *The parlour fireplace as it looked before a weekend's hard labour.*

BELOW *The restored fireplace: a slate surround and mantelpiece with details picked out in gilt, fine cast-ironwork and a set of lily-patterned ceramic tiles. It is completed with a cast-iron canopy and grate, and set off by a lovely brass fender and accessories found at Phil Lynas's fireplace shop.*

staircases

PREVIOUS PAGES *An oak staircase from the Arts and Crafts period. The hand rail fixed to the wall matches the one supported by the widely spaced balusters.*

RIGHT *The stripey woven runner and dragged green paintwork on this little staircase give a smart contemporary feel to the entrance hall. The thick velvet curtain at the front door is in keeping with the period, and also helps to keep draughts at bay.*

he decorative role of the staircase had been exploited in grand houses for a long time, but it was not until the eighteenth and nineteenth centuries that staircases became an important feature in more modest homes. As incomes rose and architectural pattern books came into more common use, the concept of new or fashionable style took off in a big way. As more importance was placed on making the 'right impression', the staircase became a symbol of wealth, conveniently placed so that it could be seen from the front door. It is often the case, however, that most of the fine timber and decoration stops at the first floor, and by the time you reach the servants' quarters on the second floor there is a very simple dog-leg staircase of painted pine.

Georgian staircases were elegant affairs with graceful hardwood hand rails, usually of mahogany, slender, turned wood balusters or fancy ironwork balustrades, and no large decorative newel post to spoil the line. During the Regency the emphasis was on simplicity of line, with a mahogany hand rail sweeping down to a swirl at the bottom of the stairs, supported by close-set, straight wood or iron balusters.

The Victorians made much more elaborate staircases. Even fairly humble terraced houses had solidly constructed staircases with newel posts and hand rails of mahogany, which was imported from the colonies. Towards the end of that era, the Arts and Crafts movement had a major influence on house style and the oak that its protagonists favoured was used, and left unpainted, for country-style staircases. Oak was expensive, though, and the fashion was limited to those who could afford it. Most Edwardian houses have staircases that are less ornate versions of high Victorian style, made of pine and mahogany.

There are several different construction styles that have been used all along, depending upon the space available. In a large, wide house the stairwell would allow for a good sweeping staircase, one that could wind around for the best effect, or include a landing. A narrower house would use a quarter-turn or half-turn staircase with landings at different levels and open space underneath. The dog-leg style was used in the narrowest houses, with rails for two floors coming off the same landing newel post and no stairwell in the middle.

In order to understand any description of making or mending a staircase it is necessary to know the names of the main components:

- **Balusters** – the individual, plain or fancy posts that support the hand rail and form a guard at the outside edge of the staircase.
- **Balustrade** – a row of balusters.
- **Glue blocks** – reinforcing triangular wedges glued behind the joints of the treads and risers, and only accessible from the back of the staircase.
- **Hand rail** – sometimes called a banister, this is the long, smooth rail on top of the balusters.
- **Newel post** – this is the first and biggest, and usually most ornate, post at the bottom of the stairs and also occurs where the stairs change direction. It is the support that is anchored to the floor.
- **Nosing** – the front edge of the tread, which is usually rounded, and usually overlaps the riser.
- **Return nosing** – a moulding, usually rounded like the nosing, that covers the outside raw edge of the tread and conceals the base of the baluster.

- **Riser** – the vertical front section between two treads.
- **Soffit** – the underside of the staircase, usually plastered over.
- **Strings** – the sides of the staircase, like skirting boards. The inner string is fixed to the wall, and the outer one holds the balusters. If the outer string is stepped to show the shape of the stairs, it is known as open string, but if it is solid it is called closed string.
- **Tread** – the horizontal part that you tread on.

All these sections are fitted together with a variety of different housings (grooves) and joints, described by names which are only 'carpenter friendly', so it is not difficult to see that this is the most complicated wooden structure in a house.

Simple stair repairs

There are a few simple stair repairs that can be managed without any special training, including stopping a creak and removing and mending balusters. For other repairs, it would be best to call in an expert.

Stopping a creak

First remove the stair carpet and walk up and down the stairs until you have located the trouble spot. The most likely cause is a loose joint between a tread and a riser, which is ideally dealt with from the back of the staircase. If this would cause major disruption – the back is usually plastered over – tackle it from the front. Follow the step-by-step guide below.

Repairing and replacing balusters

First remove the baluster by following the step-by-step guide opposite.

If the baluster is simply split, or cleanly

STOPPING A STAIR CREAK

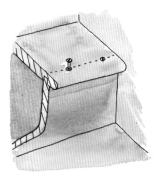

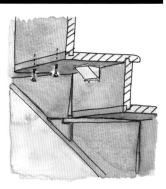

1   If you can gain access only from the front of the staircase, insert screws through the tread and into the riser along its length.

2   If you can get access from the back, remove and reposition or replace the glue block using wood glue. Slide it to and fro to add suction. Insert screws at the back of the tread, up into the riser above.

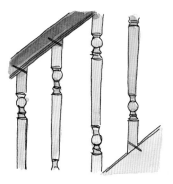 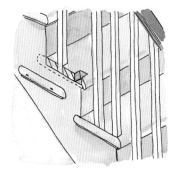

I If the balusters are butt-jointed, the base will have been cut to match the slope of the string, and nailed in place. Using a mallet, gently tap against the direction of the nailing to free the baluster. Then pull it free of the housing in the hand rail.

2 On an open string staircase, first prise off the return nosing with a hammer and chisel. Then tap the other side of the baluster to free it from the housing; and pull free of the hand rail.

broken, it may be possible to repair it. To mend a split, first make sure the split wood is clean and free of dust. Then spread a thin, even layer of glue on both surfaces and clamp them together with a G-clamp, or wrap tightly with masking tape to apply pressure, until dry.

To mend a broken baluster, first drill a hole through both pieces and insert a length of 9mm dowel to strengthen your repair. Then apply wood glue to the dowel and the broken edges and exert pressure with masking tape or a clamp until the glue has set.

If the baluster is badly damaged, take it along to a timber yard or DIY store, where you may find an exact replica. Many Victorian and Edwardian styles are back in production. They are not expensive to buy and a new baluster will be stronger than one that has been repaired. If you cannot match the original, take it to a carpenter who has a lathe and get it copied. Fix the baluster back in place by

reversing the procedure you followed to remove it, using wood glue in all housings and joints.

Replacing a staircase

If you want to replace the staircase, or even if you want to fit one into an extension and are planning to match the period features in the house, you must obtain Building Regulations Approval. This could be problematic, because the Regulations are very specific and do not allow for the individuality of old buildings. They stipulate, for example, that there has to be no more than a 42° pitch, that here has to be a 2m height clearance throughout the staircase, that all risers and treads must be the same width and height, and that the hand rail should be no less than 84cm high, but not more than 1m above the pitch. It is obvious that many of these requirements will be impossible to meet, since they are designed for new houses.

RIGHT *A fine example of a Victorian staircase. The large acorn-shaped newel post and polished hand rail are mahogany while the rest of the staircase is made from painted pine. The decorative fretwork below the return nosing has been cleverly emphasized by picking it out in a darker colour; and a stripe of even darker colour has made more of a feature of the deep skirting boards.*

So, what is the owner of an old house to do? The best advice is to enlist the help of your local Conservation Officer, who will know whether you are likely to get a sympathetic hearing from the Building Inspector, and whether there are ways in which the inspector could be satisfied that your planned staircase 'afforded safe passage' (the basic requirement) even though it does not obey the letter of the law. Waivers are granted in some cases. It is not advisable simply to go ahead without the necessary approval, because an inspector has the power to make you remove the unapproved staircase, at your own expense.

The cost of having a new staircase built from scratch is high because of the complex joinery involved. A better solution is to buy a standard prefabricated staircase from a DIY store and employ a carpenter to install it for you. It is unlikely to fit without adjustment and the carpenter may have to add, for example, a landing at the base of the flight to take account of the higher ceiling heights in Victorian and Edwardian houses. For any older house you should seek expert advice from the Georgian Society or the SPAB (see page 186).

Entire staircases can be bought from architectural salvage yards. Make sure anything that you buy is appropriate for the style and date of your house. Do not be tempted to fit an Art Nouveau staircase into an early Victorian house, for example, just because it looked tempting in the salvage yard. Needless to say, any reclaimed wooden staircase should be thoroughly checked before purchase for rot, worm and general deterioration, so take your joiner along for an expert opinion.

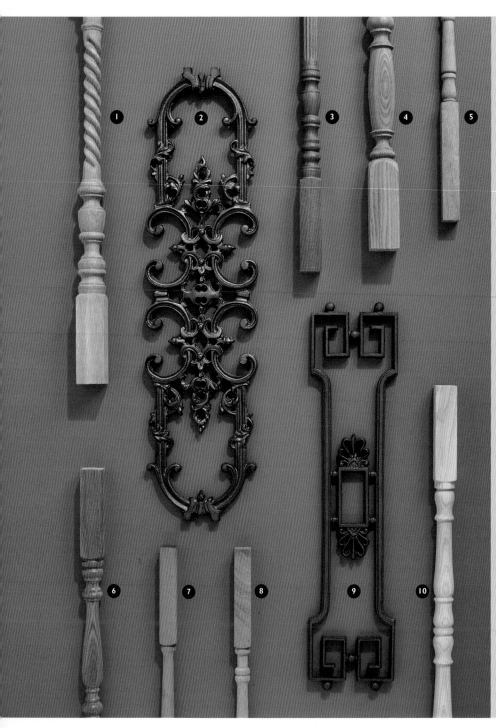

Reproduction Balusters

1 **Wooden barleytwist** *(Georgian)*
2 **Fancy cast iron** *(Victorian)*
3 **Wooden baluster – taken from a sixteenth-century pattern** *(All periods)*
4 **Wooden baluster** *(Victorian)*
5 **Wooden baluster** *(Regency)*
6 **Wooden baluster** *(Edwardian)*
7 **Wooden baluster** *(Victorian)*
8 **Wooden baluster** *(Georgian)*
9 **Cast-iron baluster** *(Georgian/Regency)*
10 **Wooden baluster** *(Victorian)*

Metal staircases

Cast-iron spiral staircases were used in Victorian public buildings, or large houses with libraries or conservatories. The patterns were highly decorative and there is still a big demand for any that are salvaged. Metal stairs would not normally have been used indoors but, being a contained unit, they can be fitted and removed quite easily. They can look fabulous and save space at the same time.

Decorative treatments

Only mahogany, oak or other fine hardwoods would have been considered worthy of showing off until relatively recently. In the past softwoods such as pine were always painted.

Fashions and patterns in staircases changed a lot throughout the eighteenth and nineteenth centuries, so it impossible to generalize about existing decoration. If you have a Georgian masterpiece that needs restoring it is worth getting the hand rail professionally French polished. If you have a more ordinary hand rail, use a good selection of wood-restoring products to clean and repolish the wood yourself. If paint has clogged the detail on balusters or string brackets, consider stripping them back to the bare wood and repainting them. However, if your staircase rises to three storeys, you could take a leaf out of the Victorians' book and concentrate your efforts on the section that is on view the most, as this is an extremely time-consuming and awkward job.

If your Victorian or Edwardian staircase is made of pine, perhaps with a mahogany rail and newel post, you could paint the treads and balusters in a contrasting colour to the strings and risers. Because the shape of a staircase is dramatic, it can take this kind of strong decorative treatment. Woodgraining, once used to dress pine up as more exotic wood, is back in fashion and does not have to be totally convincing to look good. Follow the step-by-step guide on page 161, and experiment with scumble glaze and different graining tools on scrap wood before you tackle the real thing.

Painting balusters is a fairly tedious job but there are now paint pads designed especially for the job. The pads are dipped into paint then wrapped and twisted around the turned wood. You need to fill in around the top and base with a brush, but the pads will save a lot of time on the main shaft.

Stair coverings

The traditional way to carpet stairs in an old house is to use a runner down the middle of the staircase rather than edge-to-edge carpeting. Runners can be held in place with stair rods or special clips, which allow them to be moved from time to time when wear on the treads begins to show. The bordering edges of the treads and risers can be painted or stripped and varnished, depending upon the decorative style of your staircase. Stair runners come in many different styles, and the striped woven type look especially good as they emphasize the shape of a staircase.

When you come to choose a stair carpet bear in mind what a hassle stairs are to vacuum. There are some good 'ethnic'-style runners based on old rug designs that can look good in old houses – and their 'busy' patterns hide wear and dirt very well. If you have neither pets nor children, you can indulge in the luxury of a deep, rich and highly impractical plain runner on your staircase – and enjoy every minute of it. Whatever carpet you choose, fit it with the best underlay that you can afford because it takes so much heavy traffic.

If your budget does not stretch to any sort of carpet, do not despair; stairs can be painted.

BELOW *A compact, dainty early nineteenth-century staircase. Using a stair carpet that tones in with the stripped and polished floorboards unifies the area, making it seem calmer and larger.*

RIGHT *A passion for fishing is expressed everywhere you look in this cottage hallway: each riser of the stripped-pine staircase has been used to feature a painting of a fishing scene.*

They can even be painted to look as if they are carpeted. Whether you choose a simple plain colour, stripes or a pattern, the same rules apply. Begin by preparing the surface by sanding or stripping, and then cleaning with a sugar soap solution. Prime with acrylic white primer and, when this is dry, draw out the guidelines using a chalky coloured pencil. You can use emulsion paint, acrylic, satinwood or wood stain. The advantage of emulsion is that it flows well and comes in sample-sized pots and a good range of bright colours. All these paints will need at least three coats of tough, clear polyurethane varnish. Special floor paints that do not need sealing are available, but they are quite pricey. Your budget and the size of your staircase will probably dictate your choice.

Begin painting at the top, working down on alternate steps. When these are dry, you can paint the others, so keeping the staircase in use as you work. Otherwise you will have to wait for the stairs to dry before you go back up. The great advantage of a painted stair carpet is that if you get fed up with it, you can always cover it with a real stair carpet when the budget allows.

floors

When you come to choose the way in which you treat the floors in your house, it should not be difficult to find a solution that not only fits comfortably with the period of your house, but also fits your lifestyle and budget. There is plenty of scope for getting a historical feel without sacrificing the freshness that a new floor covering can bring. Whether you choose to leave the floorboards bare – or paint or stencil them – or cover them with rush matting, lino, carpets or rugs, all these options have historical antecedents. The way that you treat the floor can pull everything together in a room, and does not have to cost the earth. A painted floor, for instance, is quick and cheap and can look perfect in an old house. And it is worth remembering that Oriental rugs have remained popular since they were first imported. Old rugs can be cleaned and repaired; they almost never lose their value; they fit almost anywhere and with any style of decoration.

Wooden floors

Plain, scrubbed wooden boards were not unusual in Georgian houses. Pine predominated,

PREVIOUS PAGES *A quick, cheap and easy way to turn a patched-up wooden floor into the main feature of a room is to paint it. This checkerboard in shades of grey has been sponged over to give a naïve marbled effect.*

LEFT *The floorboards here have been scrubbed and bleached for a light, matt effect that goes with the wooden furniture; interest has been added by painting and stencilling a simple border round the edges of the room.*

and cleaning it with sand and water, as they did, gave the boards a soft, silvery bloom. Elaborate stencilled patterns, often incorporating fashionable neo-classical motifs such as urns and Greek-key borders, were sometimes applied to the bare boards. The Victorians also used pine boards, but often stained them to imitate mahogany; and when used in conjunction with a carpet, the boards were sometimes painted to echo the darkest colour in the carpet. Towards the end of the nineteenth century, under the influence of the Arts and Crafts movement, light oak floorboards and parquet block floors (which had been a feature of grand houses long before the Georgian era), were favoured, and continued to be through the Edwardian period.

Sanded floorboards

Sanded and varnished or polished old wooden floorboards look fantastic, no matter what furniture you choose – they seem to go with everything. You can set the style with small carpets and scattered rugs: Chinese, Indian, Turkish, African, rag rugs or woven rush mats. If you are lucky enough to find that the floorboards in your house are original and in sound condition, choose this treatment for a good-looking, traditional and cheap flooring solution. The best way to go about sanding a floor is described on page 110.

Before you go out to hire a sander, check the condition of your floor. If heating and re-wiring have meant lifting some boards, they may need securing. If damaged boards have been repaired with new timber, see if you can replace them with matching old boards from an architectural salvage yard. Use a centre punch to bang nails well in. If there are small gaps between the boards, fill them with a special filler available from DIY stores. If the floor has shrunk, leaving larger gaps, these will need to be filled with matching wooden fillets to prevent draughts and cut down dust and noise. If there are not too many or too-big gaps, you can do this yourself by following the step-by-step guide on page 110. All grubby old wood with layers of varnish and polish looks much the same, so sand part of your boards before you buy the fillets, so that you can match the timber.

A hire shop (see page 187) will supply you with two types of sander, a large one and a smaller one to do the edges; both will come with a supply of discs and sanding sheets (you will be able to return what you don't use). They will also sell goggles and face-masks. Make sure that you fully understand the operating instructions before leaving the hire shop – and don't even think about hitting the 'on' switch without your goggles and mask on. You should be able to sand an average-sized living room over a weekend; adding three coats of varnish may take a little longer. This has to be one of the most exhausting, but ultimately most satisfying, restoration jobs that you can do. Revealing the pristine wood beneath the grime and enhancing it with varnish is sheer poetry.

Painted floorboards

Floors can be painted with any sort of household paint as long as you apply at least three coats of the toughest polyurethane varnish on top. Special floor paints are available from paint specialists, and these are worth using if you like the colours. They are designed to have a very tough finish and are good for heavy traffic areas like the hallway. There is also a

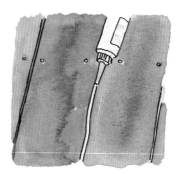

1   Before sanding, use a centre punch to sink all the nail heads below the level of the floor, to prevent damage to the sander.

2   Small gaps between boards can be filled with a proprietary filler; larger ones need filling with tapered wooden fillets.

3   The fillets will need to be cut at a carpenter's workshop, and then tapped in with a mallet and glued in position.

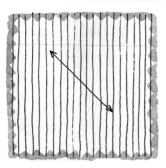

4   When using a sanding machine, work diagonally first one way then the other, then once again along the direction of the grain.

5   An edge sander should be used to reach up to the skirting boards.

6   You will need to use a file or hand sander to reach difficult areas such as those behind radiator pipes.

rubberized floor paint that is suitable for bathrooms and kitchens.

'Historic' paint ranges have been designed to complement antiques and period houses (see page 187). Consider using an historic colour like very dark green, brick red, ochre, dark 'Scandinavian' blue or even a very dark grey. Or – for a light and streaky finish – 'limewash' the wood with diluted white emulsion paint. Paint is a good way to make the floor look finished even if you intend to carpet or tile it later on, when your budget allows. It provides a quick fix that does no long-term damage – you may even find that you actually prefer the painted look to something more conventional, especially if you decide to add some form of pattern.

Patterned and stencilled floors

You do not have to be an artist to tackle painting a simple pattern on the floor; follow the basic step-by-step guide on page 112. You could stencil a striped kelim rug, an all-over pattern or a border on its own. Your house's existing decorative features may also give you ideas for patterns: there may be a design on the fireplace, a panel of stained glass or a plaster moulding whose shape could be enlarged or reduced to make a stencil.

There are also thousands of pre-cut stencils to choose from too and it is worth visiting a specialist store or sending for a mail-order catalogue to see what is on offer.

Woodstrip floors

Woodstrip is a relatively new addition to flooring options, though parquet blocks have a long history. Woodstrip consists of veneers of good hardwoods such as ash, beech, maple or oak, bonded on to a cheaper softwood backing. This can be laid on top of existing floors, as you would lay tiles. There are many different widths and lengths of board, as well as blocks, like parquet, that are felt-backed.

When choosing woodstrip, go for the thickest possible veneer to allow for sanding and re-surfacing in the future. To get the best finish, remove the skirting boards and cut away the architrave around the door to accommodate the woodstrip before you lay it; the skirtings can be replaced once the floor is down. This process is something to bear in mind when you are planning the decorative effects for the room, as moving skirting will wreak havoc with the final finish of the walls.

Carpets and soft flooring

Loomed carpets have been made since the 1740s, their patterns echoing those of the plaster decoration on the ceilings. They were, however, expensive and usually only used in the reception rooms. Wall-to-wall carpets were even more costly, as they were made to special commission, with woven borders following the shape of the room. The Victorians preferred more elaborately patterned carpets in richer, more opulent colours, until the restraining influence of the Arts and Crafts movement made itself felt; and by the early years of the twentieth century carpets had become plainer and lighter in colour. Oriental rugs continued to be extremely popular, and indeed so desirable were Turkey runners (long, narrow strips of Oriental woven carpet) in the Victorian era that the designs were copied in much cheaper mass-produced versions.

Today there is such a wide variety of carpets for every situation, from well-used stairs to little-used bedrooms, that professional advice is needed when you make your choice. Remember that good underlay extends a carpet's life, acting as a shock-absorber, and there are special heavy-duty underlays for busy areas such as the hallway and stairs. If you choose carpet for the entrance hall, ask for a mat well by the front door. This cut-out area, framed with wooden beading, holds a doormat. It not only looks neat but will save on the vacuuming. It is also worth noting that dark plain colours show specks and dirt more than light ones, as do large patterns as opposed to small ones.

Expensive carpets are best laid by professionals who have all the right tools. Cheaper foam-backed types may only need sticking down with double-sided carpet tape, and you could tackle this yourself. Sometimes a

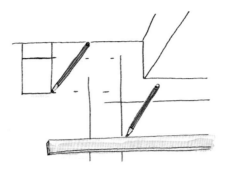

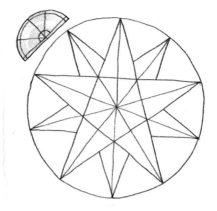

1   Sand, prime and paint the base colour on the floor. Next paint theborder. With a strip of cardboard as a measuring guide, mark and then draw the lines of the border pattern using a chalky pencil and a straight edge.

     Mark the centre and, very roughly, the size of the central motif – in this case a star.

2   Cut a length of string that will stretch from the centre of the star to the outer edge of one point. Attach one end to a drawing pin in the floor at the centre of the star, and the other to a pencil. Draw a circle using the string as the radius. Now place a protractor in the centre and mark off 36° sections – you will get ten in all. Draw the lines to the edges of the circle and then connect them up to make the star.

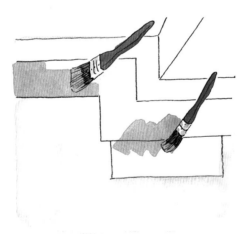

3   If you are blessed with a steady hand, fill in the stripes freehand with a medium-sized household brush. If not, you may find it easier to make a crisp edge either by running strips of masking tape along the edges or by holding a piece of card along the lines as a guide. Paint from the outer edge inwards.

4   Add stars in the borders with a stencil. Draw the star on a piece of stencil card or clear stencil plastic and cut out the pattern with a craft knife. Spray the back of the stencil lightly with spray adhesive. Paint with a flat-ended brush using a stippling or swirling movement, working from the edges inwards.

ABOVE **One of Home Front's most popular features involved the presenter, Tessa Shaw, helping to paint a pattern and border on this painted floor. Three shades of the same colour were used, giving a very calm, harmonious effect. The whole floor was painted the lightest shade of blue, then a big star motif in deeper hues was carefully plotted and then painted freehand as the centrepiece. A deeper border stripe was added, just in from the edge of the room, on to which small stars were stencilled at key points to tie in with the big star.**

good bargain carpet and a couple of rolls of tape can provide the perfect uplift for a well-worn small room – as well as for its restorer.

The concept of using sisal, sea grass, hemp or jute for flooring is far from new – woven rush matting has been used for hundreds of years – but modern technology has changed production methods completely. These very low-tech materials have been given the high-tech treatment; they can now be fitted like

carpets, wall-to-wall in wonderful colour combinations; they can be made soft enough for bare feet or tough enough for a busy airport lounge. They complement period style and lend themselves perfectly as a background for colourful Oriental rugs.

Floor cloths were, and still are, a practical and cheap solution to flooring, especially in areas such as hallways and kitchens that need a hard-wearing surface. They can be made exactly as they were throughout the nineteenth century, by applying several coats of primer to thick canvas, which can be painted in any pattern and then varnished. Imitation inlaid marble or stone, or patterns derived from Oriental rugs, were particular favourites. Using a ready-made stencil is perhaps the easiest way to achieve a good pattern today.

Floor cloths were the forerunners of linoleum, which in fact has been in production for over 150 years. Its popularity peaked in the

1950s but so, unfortunately, did the stiletto heel, which sank in and pitted the smooth surface. Subsequently it fell from favour, but now it is back, in a tougher version, and designers are taking advantage of the fantastic colour range in custom-built patterned floors that are warm, soft and 100 per cent natural. The Walshes chose lino for their kitchen and were delighted with the result. One word of warning – the price may surprise you, it is nowhere near as cheap as vinyl and must be laid by a professional on a totally flat surface.

Cork has also been in use since the nineteenth century, when it was sometimes used as an insulating, backing material for floor cloths. It deserves its current popularity because of its natural mellow colouring, and because it is comfortable underfoot and sound- and shock-absorbent. It is also easy to clean. Lay the tiles on a level surface, which can be of levelling compound or hardboard. The more expensive variety come ready-sealed, but for economy you can lay unsealed tiles and apply two or three coats of tough varnish. You can enliven the tiles by scattering them with rugs (held firm with non-slip backing strips); or by staining half the tiles black and laying them in a checkerboard pattern, which looks particularly good in a country-style kitchen.

Stone and tiled floors

Flagstones, slate and marble floors have a long history. Today the real thing is prohibitively expensive but, happily, good quality imitations are available. So good, in fact, are reproduction flagstones that only an expert eye could spot the difference. Made from concrete in moulds taken from worn flagstones, they are available in eleven different sizes (for a realistically haphazard effect) and they are half the price of the genuine article.

If you have a flagstone floor that has sunk in places you can lift the individual stones and re-bed them in sand or bedding mortar. If a stone is deeply worn – flagstones do show the passage of time – it would be a shame to tamper with it unless it is absolutely necessary from a safety point of view. If flagstones need cleaning, try scrubbing them with a solution of two tablespoons of washing soda in a nine-litre bucket of warm water; tougher waxy stains should shift with a cup of soda in a bucket of water to which a squeeze of detergent has been added.

Slate tiles were sometimes used in kitchens; their colour can be brought back by rubbing in a mixture of one part linseed oil to four parts white spirit. Leave this to permeate the surface, then wipe off any excess with a soft cloth and buff to a shine.

Inlaid marble floors featured in very grand houses throughout the eighteenth and nineteenth centuries. Good-quality imitations can produce similar effects today, and are particularly suitable for imposing hallways.

Tiles

Although clay tiles have been in use for hundreds of years, it was not until machinery produced uniform, affordable tiles in the mid-nineteenth century that their use became widespread. Quarry tiles were used for kitchen flooring, and geometric mosaics of encaustic coloured tiles were often used in Victorian and

Edwardian conservatories, pantries, bathrooms and hallways, and for front paths, .

Encaustic tiles were first used in medieval churches, and then reintroduced during the Gothic Revival period when Victorian architects looked back to the Middle Ages for inspiration. The little tiles were pressed out of moulds and fired, then coloured slips were poured in to make the decoration and they were fired a second time. If you imagine the grime that existed on the streets before the days of proper roads, pavements and sanitation, you will appreciate how very resilient these tiles were to hobnail boots and the dirt brought in with them. Not only did they endure constant cleaning in those days, but a lot have survived

LEFT *Glowing polished floorboards and a Turkey runner look perfect and make very practical flooring for the hallway of this large family house. The stair carpet gives an unfussy contemporary feel. The fixing of stair rods is decorative and practical; they allow the carpet to be moved when wear shows on the nosing. The view through to the kitchen gives a glimpse of the flagstone floor.*

the wear and tear of another 150 years. The best polish to use for encaustic tiles is a mixture of three parts boiled linseed oil to one part beeswax. But please do note that this polish must never be put on top of existing polish or the floor will turn into a skid pan. The floor must be stripped of all previous coatings for the polish to be effective and safe.

Encaustic floor tiles are now being made again, using the same types of clays, slips and processes, so it may be possible to buy matching tiles to repair a damaged floor. If you have a floor that is extensively damaged, it is well worth getting it restored by a professional.

Quarry tiles look especially good in an older-style kitchen, but they have certain drawbacks that you should bear in mind: they are cold and noisy to walk on, and nothing breakable will survive being dropped on them. If you have an old quarry-tiled kitchen floor in need of repair, you will find that new tiles, though they are made to the same standard size, are not as thick, so you will need to build up the difference with extra tile cement.

A new tiled floor must be laid on a level surface: use a levelling compound or sheets of hardboard to achieve this. Quarry tiles are especially heavy and should not be laid on anything other than a concrete base and bedding mortar. If you cannot resist laying them upstairs, and you know that the floor will take the extra weight, use chipboard as a base over the existing floor rather than hardboard, which would definitely bow.

kitchens

PREVIOUS PAGES *A mixture of traditional farmhouse fixtures and individual style is at work here. Brass taps protruding from a splashback made from a large slab of stone, a deep butler's sink and generously substantial wooden worktops make a personal statement as well as a practical kitchen.*

RIGHT *An eclectic selection of furniture, pictures and ornaments – on the period fireplace – combine with a large modern radiator and good overhead lighting to make this dining end of a kitchen a place to linger in.*

the reality of kitchens before the introduction of electricity and gas was a far cry from our romanticized view of them. Few people today would relish cooking on a coal-fired range, or turning trivets and lifting the heavy pots that hung on chains above open fires. Kitchens in ordinary homes were usually small and the only people who ate at the kitchen table were the servants. Families ate in the dining room. The idea of entertaining in the kitchen would have been shocking and impractical; it was only in the socially more relaxed atmosphere of the 1960s that the pleasures of kitchen entertaining were discovered. Small kitchens, either in the basement or at the back of the house, were extended or knocked through to the dining room to give more space and make a large family room where the cooking takes place at one end, but is not an isolated activity. This is reminiscent of the old farmhouse-style kitchen; people use the table for other things when mealtimes are over; music plays, people chat to one another and on the telephone – kitchens are the new living rooms.

Since there is little point in the pursuit of Georgian or Victorian authenticity in the modern kitchen, do the next best thing and combine the best of new labour-saving equipment with kitchen furniture that is in sympathy with the room and the rest of the house. This could mean having a carpenter build special units or adapting some ready-made ones. You may consider using individual pieces of furniture to counteract the uniformity of a designed kitchen – or using a mixture of fitted and free-standing units.

A glance through the advertisements at the back of any traditional home-decorating magazine will present you with a wide variety of bespoke-kitchen makers and suppliers of traditional fixtures and fittings. The nostalgia market has never been better catered for, with original designs being copied to a very high standard while incorporating the advantages of new technology. The kitchen has revived our respect for craftsmanship and put the creativity back into carpentry.

If you are starting from scratch but want your kitchen to blend with the rest of your old house, take your time, looking at as many styles as possible before making any decisions. It is a good idea to make up a file or scrapbook with pictures of kitchens that you like. Clip pieces of fabric, colour samples, photographs and written notes together until you get a picture of what it is that you want. If you can afford to employ a designer, he or she will understand exactly what you are after with visual clues like this, even if they are used only as a starting point, to eliminate the things that you definitely do not like. Remember that the kitchen is likely to take a bigger slice of your budget than any other individual room, so it is important to get it right.

As a general rule, you get what you pay for – and this is especially true if you are buying it new. So, if you want a beautifully made wooden kitchen, it will be expensive and is unlikely to be mass-produced or instantly available. New appliances are expensive and some big kitchen suppliers include them in their price as an incentive. If this is the case, make sure that they are the type that you want: it is all too easy to be swayed by a convincing salesman.

For most people the cost of a custom-built kitchen would be prohibitive. However, the

boom in off-the-shelf fitted kitchens over the past twenty-five years means that there is now a great variety of attractive designs available. If you feel that their standardized look would not suit the period style of your house, consider adding mouldings or changing the handles or hinges.

One way of getting the best of both worlds is to buy the shells of the units off the shelf and have a carpenter make up special doors and worktops and fit them for you. This is the way the Walshes had their kitchen done and it was a great success. They also bought their new kitchen appliances at auction, which saved a great deal of money.

Kitchen styles

Once the decorative potential of the kitchen was recognized, whether or not it was large enough to double as a living room, appropriate styles of treatment evolved, artfully combining the practicalities with the aesthetically pleasing. The country kitchen look, the painted kitchen and the Shaker-style kitchen – with many combinations and variations – all blend comfortably with a period-feel house. If you are lost in the wilderness of interior design talk, a few basic pointers to achieving different styles will be helpful. These, however, are the basic ingredients – your own blend of flavourings will give your kitchen its particular character.

Country pine style

Think rustic and assemble individual pieces of furniture rather than going for a completely fitted pine kitchen; the effect will be far more welcoming and relaxed. If you can afford to, have some built-in units made of reclaimed pine, which will blend well with old pine chairs and accessories. If you already have built-in units with melamine fronts, you can get pine replacement doors fitted. Use antiquing wax to dull the colour of new pine. A lovely old table with a scrubbed top and turned legs is the ideal centrepiece. Surround it with an assortment of kitchen chairs – a mixture of styles looks less contrived than a matching set. An old dresser, groaning with a display of antique china, is the ideal, but if it is financially out of reach, make one up simply and cheaply by running shelves above a base unit. Leave them plain or dress up the shelf edges with mouldings and the top with an architrave. If you add sides to the shelves, you can make these more interesting by cutting curved profiles with a jigsaw.

The floor can be of quarry-tiles, stripped boards, cork or, best of all, flagstones if it will bear the weight. You can now get imitation flags that are almost indistinguishable from the real thing but are, of course, much cheaper. It is essential to seal all floor surfaces to protect them against inevitable spills.

If you have the space and the budget, a traditional kitchen range is the ideal choice for the country pine kitchen. Otherwise, opt for a solid-looking free-standing cooker. Deep enamel-coloured tiles or wood with marble insets (obtained as offcuts from a marble mason) would look good on the worktops.

Lighting should be bright and functional, with spotlights used to illuminate the work areas, and perhaps enamel-shaded lights hung low over the dining table. A wooden plate-rack over a porcelain butler's sink, a fretwork corner cupboard and a set of French enamel storage jars, plenty of utensils hanging from cup hooks and lots of open shelves will all enhance the country look. So, too, will gingham or patchwork curtains and cushion covers, but avoid the brand-new, too frilly or totally co-ordinated look.

This is a busy-looking, lived-in kitchen for fridge magnets and children's artwork, notice boards, old photographs, rocking chairs and colourful rugs. The more you add, the richer it will look.

Painted country style

This look can be as contemporary or traditional as you choose, depending upon how you dress up the basic style and is particularly suited to smaller kitchens.

The core product is matchboarding – or tongue-and-groove boards. This was a popular 'below stairs' style in the Victorian and Edwardian eras, so it is well suited to an old house. Use matchboarding to line the walls up to either halfway or two-thirds of the room height. See the step-by-step instructions on page 74. Top with a shallow shelf, which will finish off the edges and provide practical and decorative shelf space.

Buy kitchen units as shells without doors and fit them with custom-made matchboard fronts. These can be ledged and braced, or simply reinforced with a couple of horizontal battens. Fit them with unfussy black iron hinges and latches. In the past this type of boarding would have been painted with gloss for easy cleaning, but matt colours make a more sympathetic finish.

Colours can be light creamy yellows, mint greens or pale blues. Fabrics in tartan, checks or stripes in mellow colours that pick up the background wall and cupboard colour will add character and soften the hard edges. If you fit a butler's sink, use the same fabric for a curtain below; avoid cupboards here because water inevitably drips down the shiny sink surface, and will eventually cause wood to rot.

Natural wood worktops, and sanded and varnished floorboards or cork or terracotta tiled floors complete the look. Leave the floors bare for easy sweeping or cover them with rush mats, rugs or dhurries, held in place by non-slip rubber underlay to avoid accidents. The basic kitchen has a puritanical simplicity that can be dressed up with open shelves, baskets, bunches of dried flowers, herbs and spices and collections of crockery.

Shaker style

The beauty of Shaker design arises from simple lines, fine craftsmanship, and an insistence on the purposefulness of objects. The Shakers were a religious sect who set up a style of communal living in north-east America in the mid-nineteenth century. Their rigid moral principles were applied to every aspect of living, from sexual celibacy to built-in cupboards. Nowadays people talking about Shaker design seem to do so with a quasi-religious fervour, so their influence lives on.

True Shaker style has 'a place for everything, and everything in its place'. They built cupboards into the walls, kept small items in stacking boxes and fitted hanging peg-rails at picture-rail height around all their rooms. In the evening all chairs were hung from the rails to clear the floors for sweeping and 'shaking' – their ritualistic form of dance during worship. They favoured fruit- and maplewood as construction materials for their simple, beautifully crafted furniture, which was polished or painted with flat colour. Fabrics, in natural

materials, were checked, striped or plain, in the same colour palette as the paintwork.

You can give your kitchen a Shaker look by running a wooden peg-rail around the walls, banishing clutter and painting plain units a flat colour. The colours to choose are dark and light blue, blue-green, buttermilk yellow, brick red or cherry red. Use matt colour only and contrast it with round wooden handles or pegs, either by leaving them as natural wood or by painting them a paler or darker colour. Several companies are now making milk paints in the original styles and colours (see page 187).

Floors in Shaker-style kitchens should be wooden, as should the worktops, the latter ideally in ash. Think plain and keep all lines vertical or horizontal. There are shops that import furniture and accessories directly from the Shaker heartland in America, and kitchen suppliers offer Shaker style across the whole spectrum of price and quality.

Victorian Gothic style

This decorative approach is perfectly suited to houses of the Victorian Gothic Revival period, but it is also the sort of kitchen where weird and wonderful dishes are cooked up to be eaten by the light of a blazing Gothic candelabra. It is for people with a taste for high drama, who live in unusual houses and have relatively little interest in practical work surfaces or microwave ovens.

Do not attempt to install this style in one go, but allow it to evolve as you come across more and more interesting 'finds'. Start by visiting an architectural salvage yard, particularly one that deals in church salvage. Here you may find the beginnings of a Gothic look: church pews, carved and fretted shelves and perhaps a stained-glass panel or two. Keep an eye out for

suitable handles, hinges and brass light fittings, as well as glass-fronted wall cupboards, and a solid old table.

You could dress up fitted units with carved mouldings, then paint them in a Gothic colour: olive green, gold, purple, crimson or deep ultramarine blue. An old deep butler's sink would look well in this sort of setting; and use Victorian Gothic patterned tiles, or plain white tiles edged in dark stained wood, for worktops and splashbacks. The biggest asset in a kitchen such as this would be an original cast-iron range – gleaming black with glowing embers. Alternatively, try to find a stove that has a dark enamelled finish.

Seek out old apothecaries' jars for food storage – the ones that are labelled Arsenic and Belladonna are in such demand that reproductions are now available. Bristol-blue glass jars, cast-iron kettles and porcelain jelly

moulds will look right, as will a collection of old enamelware or tins. You can complete the look with Gothic wallpaper, stencils and rubber stamps, arched wallpaper friezes and wrought-iron accessories. Lace along shelf edges and at the windows will soften the effect, but is still in keeping with the basically ecclesiastical style. Finally, hang a big Gothic-style candelabra over the table, and use candlesticks for added moodiness at night.

Adapting an existing modern kitchen

The one type of kitchen that looks completely out of place in an old house is the total re-fit in wipe-clean melamine or Formica with aluminium trim. So what can you do if you buy a house that has one of these, in perfectly good order, and your budget is tight?

For a start, the units can be painted. Give them a good rub-down with sandpaper, then a matt oil-based undercoat. Follow this with a topcoat chosen from one of the traditional colour ranges and impose a new style by adding wooden or wrought-iron handles. Replace Formica with tiles and disguise existing unattractive tiles with paint. There is a good paint called Tile Primer by Craig & Rose (see page 187) that acts as a matt base coat, allowing a coat of gloss to key in well. If you paint the tiles with white gloss, they can then be individually stencilled or stamped with motifs of your choice.

Wooden floors can be sanded and varnished or painted. Ugly vinyl can be temporarily hidden with cheap grass mats held in place with non-slip rubber underlay.

Kitchens in old houses benefit from an eclectic look, so mix old with new. Use open shelves to show off nice tins, and hang utensils from a rail within arm's reach. Buy an old towel rail and traditional glass cloths and a wooden dish drainer instead of a plastic one. Try to see this type of inherited kitchen as a challenge – and rise to it.

Kitchen ranges

The Aga was invented in the 1920s and has become a design classic, achieving cult status, with its presence almost guaranteeing the saleability of your house.

The original Agas were coal-fired. Today they operate on most fuels, including bottled gas and off-peak electricity. Buying an Aga is not straightforward – your house will have to be assessed for suitability, but nine out of ten houses get the go-ahead. A technical team will look at the strength of your floor (that amount of cast iron is very heavy) and decide on the type of flue you will need. Formerly you needed a conventional chimney flue, but you can now have a balanced flue if the Aga is fitted to an outside wall. Another new development – a motorized extractor that can be fitted to an inside flue – means that an Aga can be fitted to an inside wall. The flue can be channelled inside the house to a suitable outside wall and vented there. The size of your kitchen is also important: it needs to be big enough to take the heat that is generated by an Aga, otherwise it will be unbearably hot.

Many companies restore old Agas, but as Agas are practically indestructible, even the second-hand price is quite high. One reason for this is that the ranges have to be fitted by experts, and it takes two people at least a full day to do it.

The Raeburn is the little sister of the Aga and is more suited to small kitchens. It has the added advantage of being fitted to a back boiler, which can heat radiators and also provide hot water.

Both Agas and Raeburns come in a range of enamelled colours, but for purists the old cream one reigns supreme.

Traditional black kitchen ranges, both restored old ones and new reproduction ones, are available from some specialist companies (see page 187), who will also have the expertise to fit them for you, as they require a chimney with a Grade 1 flue. If you have set your heart on owning one of these but don't fancy stoking the fire, they can be fitted with a coal-effect, gas-powered fire that looks just like the real thing – and you can keep your microwave oven hidden in a cupboard.

Kitchen ranges were made to local designs, so, for example, the Yorkshire range is different from the Cornish range, and they come in all sizes – not all are enormous. Make inquiries locally through fireplace suppliers and you may find one that is perfectly suited to your house. Though few people would actually cook all their meals on an old-fashioned range these days, and any time-travelling Victorian cook would consider us crazy even to think of it, they are romantic, nostalgic appliances from another age, and will charm all your visitors on a cold winter's night.

RIGHT *A classic cream enamel range surrounded by a collection of old ephemera makes a kitchen that is in keeping with a period house, especially one decorated in a nostalgic style. The cream and green colour scheme is very traditional but has been given a refreshing lift by the crisp, plaid-patterned curtains.*

THE WALSHES' KITCHEN

When the Walshes bought their house, the kitchen was a small room with a back door to the garden and a side door to the dining room. Maxine immediately wanted to knock down the dividing wall and make a big kitchen/diner, but Graham liked the idea of keeping a separate cooking area. The discovery of a huge, original cast-iron kitchen range in the kitchen chimney breast made Graham think again. After all, if you have a feature like that you don't want it hidden from view. With the help of designer Peter Plaskitt and architect Suzanne White, they eventually reached a compromise, opting for a large open hatch between the kitchen and dining room.

Since the hatch was being made in a supporting wall, an RSJ (reinforced steel joist) had to be inserted to take the weight of the upper floors.

Peter Plaskitt had a plate-rack made up to fit into the hatch, so that plates can be reached from both sides, and there is still a large open space that allows a view from one room into the other.

The decision to keep the range also involved a certain amount of compromise, because even if the Walshes had been able to afford the necessary expensive refurbishment, they still would not have wanted to do their cooking on it. It has stayed as a purely decorative feature, professionally sandblasted *in situ* to clear it of rust, and fitted with a replacement door.

The kitchen units were basic off-the-shelf shells that were customized by a joiner and then painted. Turned wooden details, made by cutting a baluster in half, and chunky white ceramic door knobs were added.

The Walshes opted for ash worktops, but Peter Plaskitt persuaded an initially dubious Maxine to include one granite work surface –

which they bought as an offcut for a very reasonable price – around the hob.

The Walshes went to an auction for their dark green enamelled gas cooker and hob, which they got at a knock-down price. They indulged themselves, however, with handmade tiles for the splashback. The wallpaper set the colour scheme for the units, the tiles, and the lino flooring – deep red and ochre.

The floor space in the kitchen is small and the Walshes were able to use a lino offcut, which was fitted by Maxine's uncle, with a cut pattern to echo the motif on the wallpaper.

LEFT *Clever shopping meant that the Walshes were able to afford to mix luxuries, such as the granite work surface, with bargains like the saleroom stove.*

TOP *The kitchen range as it looked when it was first uncovered.*

RIGHT *Designer Peter Plaskitt helped the Walshes get exactly what they wanted into a tiny kitchen. Natural materials like the wooden cupboards and lino on the floor make a sympathetic setting for the huge, cast-iron range that was retained as a showpiece.*

bathrooms

a special room for washing was not included in houses until the mid-nineteenth century, although some very rich households had water piped from roof tanks as early as 1800. The bathroom proper only made its appearance in the late nineteenth century with the invention of the circulatory hot water system, using the heat of the kitchen range to heat water in a back boiler that fed into a system of pipes. With this development, the bath could be fixed in one place.

We are so clean, and so reliant on taps and flushes in the developed world today, that it is hard to understand why it took our ancestors so long to invent the bathroom. Despite the opulence of much architecture, furniture and ornament, standards of personal hygiene remained primitive until the mid-Victorian era. Then, with towns and cities growing at a tremendous rate and after several serious epidemics of cholera, the need for a law to enforce basic standards of hygiene became clear. The Public Health Act of 1848 covered drainage, ventilation and sanitation. Gradually loos, sinks and baths began to be put in all new houses. The advances in one decade – the 1880s – were quite amazing: radiators, heated towel rails, overhead and full-body showers, steam baths and syphonic flushing WCs appeared in all shapes and sizes. The first bathrooms were decorated like bedrooms, but steam soon became a problem because it ruined wallpapers and fabrics. It was not until the invention of the mixer-tap around 1900 that clouds of steam were much reduced. In the meantime the Victorian obsession with hygiene and cleanliness had led to the design of a smooth-enamelled cast-iron bath with no crevices to harbour germs. The development of a more reliable hot-water supply encouraged bathroom design to take off during the

Edwardian period. Luckily for us, builders seem to have been reluctant to destroy the fixtures and fittings that they removed when they were modernizing or demolishing old houses and many whole bathroom suites, as well as individual pieces and fittings, can be found at specialist dealers and in salvage yards.

Georgian houses had no special bathrooms, but many subsequently had them put into existing or specially built back extensions. If you are very lucky you may find an original Victorian bathroom still intact, and you may find an Edwardian house which still has all the original fittings and fixtures. Unfortunately you are far more likely to discover that the whole lot has been ripped out and replaced with something in olive green, turquoise or pastel pink plastic, with water-splash-effect tiling. This was the most popular style for bathroom replacements in the late 1960s and 1970s and the evidence remains to haunt us.

The decorative options open to you for bathrooms in a period house are as wide as they are for kitchens. There is no reason why you should not fit a totally new, modern-style bathroom in an old house, if this is what you prefer. A well-designed plain white suite is preferable to a poor reproduction of a fancy old one, and you can furnish the room with a mixture of old and new objects. The eclectic look suits old houses and good design never goes out of fashion.

On the other hand, you may decide to invest in an original or reproduction period

THE HOME FRONT GUIDE

Reproduction Bathroom Accessories

1   **Ceramic tile**
    (Georgian)
2   **Barleytwist chain pull**
    (Georgian)
3   **Toilet roll holder**
    (Georgian)
4   **Nickel sponge and
    cup holder**
    (Georgian)
5   **Pewter shaving mug**
    (Georgian)
6   **Scallop soap dish**
    (Georgian)
7   **Ceramic lidded
    toothbrush dish**
    (Georgian/Victorian)
8   **Brass soap dish**
    (Victorian)
9   **Sunflower cistern
    bracket**
    (Late Victorian)
10 **Ceramic tile**
    (Victorian)
11 **Bibcock brass tap**
    (Victorian)
12 **Toilet roll holder**
    (Victorian)
13 **Long-nosed basin taps**
    (Victorian/Edwardian)
14 **Ceramic tile**
    (Victorian)
15 **Chrome ribbon toilet
    roll holder**
    (Edwardian)
16 **Chrome brush and
    razor set**
    (Edwardian)
17 **Ceramic chain pull**
    (Victorian/Edwardian)
18 **Antique nickel
    bath/shower mixer**
    (Edwardian)
19 **Chrome butterfly-wing
    soap dish** *(Edwardian)*
20 **Ceramic tile**
    (Victorian)

suite, perhaps converting one of the bedrooms to make a more spacious, less utilitarian room. If you have a large enough room, bear in mind that the bath can be centrally placed. This eliminates the problem of sealing the edge and tiling the wall. If the bathroom is well ventilated (ideally by an extractor fan) steam will not be a problem either. This really frees up your decorating style, as nothing has to be especially waterproof – except the floor, of course, particularly if you share a bathroom with young children or hearty sportsmen. If you already have a clear idea of what you like, you only need to go out and find it; otherwise it is a good idea to look through home-style magazines and bathroom catalogues to get a good idea of what is on offer.

Original period fittings

Many specialist bathroom shops sell restored original suites and fittings, ranging from a modest toothbrush holder to hugely expensive Edwardian bath and shower combinations. Architectural salvage yards usually have cast-iron roll-topped baths, sinks and brass fittings, but not necessarily in matching sets. If you are buying from a salvage yard it is important to choose a bath with good enamel, because resurfacing is expensive and may cost a lot more than your bath. And since cast-iron baths are usually sold without the taps, make sure you find a set to fit at the same yard. Be warned: they can cost as much again and push the bath beyond your budget.

Some architectural salvage companies deal exclusively in bathrooms and they will be able to advise you on the conversions that are needed to use old fixtures with modern plumbing and hot-water systems, and of the weight restrictions for heavy cast-iron baths. Your floors must be capable of taking the

weight of the bath, plus around 110kg in water weight and your own weight as well. If you have doubts it is best to consult a structural engineer, or ask the building surveyor who originally checked the house for you.

It is very important to understand about plumbing regulations or to buy from someone who does. Be particularly careful about buying bathroom fixtures abroad; they have different-sized pipes and the conversion to make them compatible will be costly. Some old taps cannot be used with the latest gas boilers; and some hot-water tanks do not have the capacity to fill a big, deep bath. A reputable salvage dealer, such as those belonging to SALVO, should alert you to such problems, but they are in the business of selling things, so do your homework before you go.

The repro option

There is a tremendous range of reproduction bathroom fixtures and fittings on sale, many made from the original patterns and materials. It is worth looking at salvage, first, however, before you make up your mind to go for a reproduction, because you will be better able to judge the quality if you have already seen the real thing. Reproduction bathrooms range from the simple, plain and quite cheap to the fantastically ostentatious and expensive. They combine the styling and detailing of the past with all the advantages of modern technology. Because the bathroom is such a tactile area, manufacturers have realized that just looking like the real thing from a distance is not good enough – things have to feel real, too. Baths must be enamelled, taps made of solid brass, and loo seats wooden and generously cut.

If possible, visit one of the top-of-the-range reproduction bathroom showrooms, a mid-range specialist shop and a DIY superstore, to

LEFT *Every feature of this turn-of-the-century bathroom, from the fireplace to the Lincrusta walls, Turkish carpets and period bath and loo, spells luxury on a grand scale. Give a spare bedroom this treatment and you will never want to get out of the tub.*

get a good overview of what is available. They will all offer bathroom planning and design advice and you should come away with armfuls of brochures, price lists and planning grids. If you cannot get to a showroom, write to The British Bathroom Council (see page 187); their fact files contain plenty of good information and advice.

You may want to re-create the early twentieth-century style – with tiles to shoulder or ceiling height, and bath and basin boxed in. The Edwardians were very keen on built-in furniture because it cut down on cleaning. There are plenty of reproduction ceramic tiles to choose from, some still in production by the original companies. Try to mix some genuine old pieces in with good reproductions to add authenticity: you can buy old soap dishes, towel rails or frames in antique markets or junk shops.

Adapting an existing modern bathroom

If you are on a tight budget and have inherited a coloured bathroom suite that you don't like, you can make it appear less dominant by using a more highly saturated version of that colour on the walls. If it is pastel pink, for example, paint or paper the walls a very deep fuchsia pink, with more blue than orange in it. If it is olive green – which was a popular Arts and Crafts colour – choose a darker shade of the same colour for the walls and stencil a William Morris-style pattern in yellow ochre as a frieze to draw the eye upwards. Turquoise blue can become an integral part of an appropriately watery environment – use deeper blue-green and viridian or emerald green broad stripes for the walls. Do not be tempted to use contrasting colours, for they will only draw

I   Make sure that the glass is clean and grease-free. Spray a light whiff of spray adhesive on the back of the stencil to hold it on the glass.

2   Either stipple on Paint Magic's frosting medium (see page 188) or spray on matt white car spray paint to stencil on the pattern. The lightest drift of white gives the best 'etched' appearance.

attention to the colour of the suite; try and overpower the colour instead.

If the tiling is horrible, clean it with sugar soap, then paint it with Craig & Rose's Tile Primer (see page 187). This is a matt oil-based primer that gives the topcoat a good surface to key into. It takes a while to dry but can then be painted over with high gloss, or stencilled.

If the bath has a plastic side panel, replace it with a wooden one or tile a piece of board to fit. Matchboarding also looks good, and it can also be used around the walls to cover up existing tiles. Top it off with a useful shallow shelf. If you are replacing the bath panel, remember that you may need to have access to the pipes under the bath, so make a removable section to allow for this.

If you have an unattractive view and plain windows, stencil a pretty lacy pattern on the windows to make them look as though they

have been etched or sandblasted. Follow the step-by-step instuctions above. If your windows have ugly modern frosted glass, drape a length of butter muslin over them – the light will still penetrate but the pattern won't show.

Floors need to be splash-proof; well-sanded floorboards can be painted with rubberized floor paint for a quick, cheap make over.

Fill the bathroom with eye-catching things, such as collections of old bottles or shells; and cover the walls with framed pressed flowers and photographs. Enjoy a sense of triumph as the bathroom suite fades into insignificance.

Showers

Surprisingly enough, showers are not new – they pre-date fitted bathrooms. The earliest ones, in the 1840s, were curtained cubicles with a deep tray at the bottom and a shower head above. The tray was filled and the water

BELOW *A pretty, old marble washbasin has been set below utilitarian chrome taps, making an interesting juxtaposition of styles. The splashback area has been gilded in silver, as has the original built-in wardrobe reflected in the mirror.*

pumped up to fill an overhead tank which discharged its contents at the pull of a string. Once bathrooms became fitted in the 1890s, showers became more sophisticated and the ultimate in luxury was one with side jets and an overhead rose – exactly as it is today.

Showers work in different ways and it is important to get the type best suited to your needs as well as the plumbing system in your house. Thermostatic mixer showers take water from the mains and hot-water tank and mix it to a pre-set temperature. Manual mixer

showers use water in the same way but you adjust the temperature yourself. Electric showers use the cold water from the mains and heat it instantaneously. They are very economical but the temperature can be affected during very cold weather when the mains temperature is low. Power showers have an integral pump that overcomes the need for good water pressure. Before you buy one of these, check that your storage tank can fill as quickly as it empties and that the shower tray can empty as quickly as it fills. Shower curtains are inadequate for a power shower, so you will need a cubicle or, if it is combined with a bath, an enclosure not just a screen.

A shower cubicle must be sealed to the wall and the tray. It is one of the least successful DIY jobs, and there are a lot of damaged ceilings below showers to prove it. Unless you have experience it is a job best left to experts.

Adding atmosphere

It is a good idea to incorporate a softer, more relaxing light for leisurely night-time baths as well as a source of bright light to illuminate make-up and shaving mirrors. Candle sconces are perfect: they do not need electricity and can be positioned anywhere on the wall. It is essential to have any lights and other electrical appliances in the bathroom fitted by an electrician, and all light switches must, by law, be outside the room, because water and electricity are a lethal combination.

One last word on bathrooms – if you make yours out of a bedroom that has a fireplace, keep it. There can be nothing quite as luxurious as lying in a hot bubble bath in front of an open fire, sipping a glass of wine by candlelight …

ABOVE *The owner of this theatrical Victorian-style bathroom was lucky enough to find or inherit the magnificent basin which forms its centrepiece. The sense of drama has been heightened by strong contrasts: the ornate white porcelain and white-painted shelving stand out against walls which have been covered in anaglypta painted shiny black.*

THE WALSHES' BATHROOM

Maxine's first reaction to the existing bathroom was that the suite had to go. The reason that she found the bath so difficult to like was its size: being a small person, she felt completely dwarfed by it. Designer Peter Plaskitt convinced her, however, that the original Victorian china bath was a treasure. Also, although it was worth a lot of money, it would be difficult to sell, as it was very big and heavy and would have been a major liability on the staircase. So they decided to make this magnificent feature a focal point, and moved it to centre stage in the room. Unfortunately the original globe taps on the bath and basin had to go, as they were of a type that is illegal with a combi boiler (one that has no hot tank but heats water as you need it). Instead they bought reproduction antique brass taps that were suitable. These were expensive, but luckily money was saved on the modern shower which was bought, with a cubicle, in a local sale. These were installed as a separate shower unit in one corner of the room.

The basin was also original and the Walshes decided to keep it, but moved it and built a useful cupboard beneath it. They did, however, get a new loo. The existing one was an ordinary modern one and they wanted something that was similar in character to the bath and basin. Even though Maxine started out by thinking that she would not buy a second-hand toilet, they eventually found what they were looking for at a salvage yard. As a compromise they bought a new pine seat.

Once the plumbing was in place, Maxine and Graham covered the lower half of the walls with matchboarding; this concealed the piping, added insulation and gave a period feel to the room. The wooden floorboards were coated with blue acrylic floor paint.

Jocasta Innes showed the Walshes how they could make their own 'obscured glass' for privacy in a bathroom or to hide a bad view. Using a lace-patterned stencil and frosting medium, she painted the plain glass with a broad stencil brush to give a light, stippled effect. You could also use a light spraying of white aerosol paint with a stencil to obtain a similar etched effect. Jocasta stressed that the paint should be used very, very thinly. To achieve a similar effect, follow the step-by-step guide on page 142.

TOP *When they first saw the bathroom, the Walshes thought nothing was worth saving.*

RIGHT *The porcelain bath now takes centre stage and the old basin has been boxed in to match the walls. The colour scheme provides a vibrant backdrop to the star of the show.*

colours, paints and wall coverings

If you choose to decorate an old house along traditional lines, take your inspiration from the genuine article, not from somebody's watered-down version of it. Visit old houses of the same period that are open to the public, or museums such as the Jeffrye Museum in London, where authentic period room settings are displayed. Reference, art college and university libraries are real treasure troves; if you do not have access to one of these, though, try the reference section of your local library; it is likely to offer a better selection of books than the lending section.

In the end you should make decisions that please you, because you have to live in a home, not a museum or a 'set piece'. If pink is the only colour you like, then who is to say you shouldn't use it everywhere. But before you do, spend some time investigating the innumerable shades and tints of pink that are now available, perhaps 'mixing and matching' them to give depth and richness to an essentially monochrome scheme.

In the not so distant past, certain colours were either in fashion or out, but there was always cream if you could not make up your mind. (White was actually thought to be quite a Bohemian choice, associated with artists' studios and hot countries.) A quick glance at any contemporary 'interior style' magazine today, however, shows that, as with clothing, there is no single style of the times – anything goes. Paint companies have colour-mixing facilities that enable people to mix practically any colour in any finish they wish; and endless weighty sample books make choosing wallpaper a process that could seriously damage your health. What should be a great pleasure often turns sour when too much choice creates confusion. Perhaps this is why the pared-down simplicity of historic colours and traditional paints have caught people's imagination.

Georgian colours

Colours in the eighteenth century were limited by the availability of natural pigment, and paints were mixed by the house painter, not bought ready-made. Fashion was everything in Georgian society and people went to great trouble to keep up with the latest styles and colours. Favourite colours were sage green (known now as Georgian green), blue-grey, ochre, burnt umber, burgundy and red. The white used in this period was more of a stone or cream colour. Gold was used a good deal for highlighting details. Reception rooms tended to be painted in light colours and dining rooms in darker shades. Any rooms designated for the servants were cream, grey or drab brown.

Robert Adam had a major influence in the late eighteenth century when he returned from Italy, inspired by the way Italians used colour in their buildings and by the colours that survived in the ruins of Pompeii. He introduced a much brighter palette of yellow, blue, pea green, purple, ruby red. His hallmark, low-relief plasterwork, was set off by these colourful backgrounds and, again, highlighted with a lot of gold. Different colours were used to emphasize the divisions between the dado and the upper wall, and between the cornice and the ceiling, which tended to be heavily decorated in the wealthiest households.

During the short Regency period colours were generally lighter and woodwork was usually painted white. The so-called 'Regency' stripe – wide stripes of a pale colour with white which enjoyed a revival in the 1950s – sometimes featured on the walls, but as fabric not wallpaper.

THE HOME FRONT GUIDE

Georgian-style fabrics, wallpapers and paint colours

1   'Percier Damask' fabric
2   'La Musique' chintz fabric
3   'Regency Stripe' wallpaper
4+5 'Charleston' border papers
6   'Romney' wallpaper
7   'Clandon' wallpaper
8   'Opera Stripe' fabric
9   'Rosette Stripe' fabric
10 'Couronne' wallpaper
11 Striped wallpaper
12 'Sugar Bay Light' paint
13 'Drab' paint
14 'DH Stone' paint
15 'Pea' paint

LEFT *The warm duck-egg blue walls have been colourwashed in this light airy room, to give a slightly distressed finish. The pale wood floor, damask upholstery fabric, striped sofa and blind and the simple elegance of the small fireplace create a Regency mood.*

Victorian colours

Bright colours are not generally associated with the Victorian look, but they were used. Aniline dyes, made from coal tar and invented in 1856, brought about a new range of vivid colours, including chrome yellow, bright blue, brilliant pink and mauve. Other colours like viridian and crimson soon followed, and were put to good use by designers such as Augustus Pugin and William Burgess. Sadly, most Victorian households seemed to prefer more sombre colours such as deep, dark reds, greens, purples and browns, and Pugin's influence was felt more in shapes and patterns than in colours. Later in the period, William Morris and his contemporaries introduced a different colour palette; they rejected the new synthetic colours and championed 'honest' earth and vegetable pigments. Ochre, olive green, umber, sienna, light blue, sage and burgundy became more widely used, while woodwork was preferably left unpainted.

Edwardian colours

The Art Nouveau and Arts and Crafts movements had a strong influence in the Edwardian period, as did the Queen Anne Revival. The result was a diluted style, with much lighter colour schemes for homes that had the benefit of electric lighting and gas fires that did not produce the grime of coal and candles. Pastel colours were used with white or cream woodwork. As well as floral patterns on light backgrounds, wallpapers featured posies, ribbons and stripes. Favourite colours included peach, peppermint, sky blue, lemon yellow, lavender and pale grey.

Victorian-style fabrics, wallpapers and paint colours

1   William Morris 'Iris'
    wallpaper
2   'Melbury' fabric
3   'Pompadour'
    wallpaper
4   'Rhododendron'
    fabric
5   'Grand Indienne'
    fabric
6   'Evenlode' fabric
7   'Okeford' wallpaper
8   'Hamilton Hall'
    fabric
9   'Rhododendron'
    cotton lace
10 'Kensington'
    wallpaper
11 'Eating Room Red'
12 'Mahogany'
13 'Yellow Ochre'
14 'Mid Brunswick
    Green'

The new 'old' paint ranges

You may want to decorate your old house using the 'correct' paints and colours for the period. Until recently this would have meant hours of research and trips to expensive specialist paint companies who would mix the colour for you. Now you can choose from the ranges of more than a dozen suppliers of traditional paint and send away for a sample pot to check that you like it. Farrow & Ball supply the National Trust with a range of paints inspired by the original colours in their historic houses; Fired Earth have a range produced in conjunction with the Victoria & Albert Museum, and Paint Magic's historic colours are made by Scotland's Craig & Rose who have been in the paint business since 1829. Mainstream paint companies such as Crown and Dulux also produce their own historic ranges. (See pages 187–188.)

Distemper and limewash are some of the most popular paints at the moment, especially for decorating old houses, because of their ability to 'breathe'. This means that they allow damp to disperse rather than be trapped in the wall, as happens with impermeable vinyl paints. A lot of harm has been done to old buildings by people's misguided efforts to keep them dry and draught-free. Applying waterproof coatings to both the outside and inside walls, and then insulating the house thoroughly, thus preventing natural ventilation, has led to a lot of problems with damp that would not have occurred if the original type of paints had been used.

Quite apart from this, distemper has become popular for its lovely soft finish. It is a joy to paint with and takes a couple of hours to dry. The resulting colour is several shades lighter than when wet and the surface has a powdery bloom that is quite unlike that of any other type of paint finish. Limewash paints, now also being made to traditional recipes with added pigments to give a range of light colours, have equally appealing finishes. As interior designer Anne Papworth observed in the *Home Front* feature on historic paints after having her home painted with limewash: 'It looks as if it has been here for a very long time, it's instantly mellow.'

Another 'newcomer' from the past is milk paint, also known as casein paint. Its qualities have been summarized by Jocasta Innes: 'It has a matt finish, with a slight bloom, although not as much as distemper. It gives good coverage and is fast drying. Americans and Scandinavians have a tradition of using this type of paint. It is good for painting furniture, particularly rough wood, but would be an expensive way to paint walls.' It was the first water-based paint and was formulated in America in the early 1800s. Lacking the materials for making traditional European paints, the settlers experimented with earth, mineral and plant pigments using milk as a binder. The paint they invented could be used for walls, woodwork, crafts and furniture and was the first protein-bound house paint. Before that protein had been used as a binder only in the egg tempera that was used in fresco painting. Several different companies are now marketing milk paints – the most authentic 'folk' colour range, called Heritage Village Colours, is imported from the United States. The paints are perfect if you want to go for a Shaker colour scheme.

Painting woodwork

A lot of people now choose to paint woodwork with emulsion or acrylic paint, followed by a strengthening coat of clear varnish. Professional painters and decorators remain sceptical, however, and continue to use an undercoat and eggshell or gloss topcoat, and this no doubt gives greater protection. Old paints contained a lot of linseed oil and this is the reason that the wood looks so good when the paint is stripped.

A matt finish is better suited to an old house and there are some good historic colour ranges that use oil-based formulas. House painters in Victorian times used to mix a special 'flatted' colour that was fast drying and needed two men to work on the same area at the same time to get a totally smooth and sheen-free finish. There is also a 'dead flat varnish' that can be applied over any colour to give the same no-sheen effect.

One way of treating skirtings and dado rails in an old house is to apply a distressed paint finish. First paint the woodwork with a base colour and leave it to dry. Then rub candlewax along the edges of the mouldings to repel the water-based topcoat which you apply next. Alternatively, paint on the topcoat in a contrasting colour and, once dry, rub it back along the mouldings using fine wire wool or sandpaper. The effect can be as subtle or bold as you like: contrasting colours like burnt orange just showing through deep blue in places, or red through dark green look great.

When painting panelled doors, keep the brush strokes going in the direction of the construction, as described in the following extract from *Weale's House Painting, Graining & Marbling*, a decorator's handbook published in 1888.

The panels must be finished first, great care being taken to carry the paint clean into the edges and corners. The styles and framing should then be done. It is convenient to paint the muntins, or munnions, first – these are the upright pieces in the middle of the door. Next come the upper, middle and lower rails

Edwardian-style fabrics, wallpapers and paint colours

1 'Oscar' fabric
2 'Josephine' wallpaper
3 'Madame Bovary' wallpaper
4 'Florence Damask' wallpaper
5 'Pale stripes' wallpaper
6 'Rose & Ribbon' fabric
7 'Damask Fantasie' fabric
8 Anaglypta dado border
9 'Chalfont' wallpaper
10 'Humble Pie' paint
11 'Eau de Nil' paint
12 'Pale Cream' paint
13 'Heather Mist' paint

– the horizontals which cross the door, and lastly, the upright styles – or external vertical portions of the frame of the door. The brushmarks, should any appear at the parts where the work is necessarily in cross-directions, will correspond with the joins which would in reality exist in these parts. This is a perfect description of how the job should be done, and it should be followed to the letter. There are similar conventions for painting a sash window. Begin by lowering the top half of the sash, stopping within 5cm of the sill. Push the bottom sash up to the top. Paint the lowered top sash then push it back up to finish it off. Now paint the lower sash. Paint the frame and runners last and move both sashes after a few hours, to prevent them from sticking.

Special paint effects

Stencilling

Stencils were used during the Victorian and Edwardian periods and are certainly the cheapest way to apply pattern to walls. There are several books on the market that are devoted exclusively to historic patterns. Ready-made stencils are also available, as well as handbooks on stencilling. Stencils can be cut from oiled stencil card (make your own using thin card treated with a coat of knotting, a spirit-based sealant, on both sides) or a flexible plastic called Mylar. The secret of converting a pattern into a stencil is to include enough 'ties' to hold the cut design together, without allowing them to dominate. Use a photocopier to enlarge or reduce your chosen design, then spray the paper with spray adhesive and stick it to the stencil material. Cut through the pattern and the card or plastic, working in from any corners, not out towards them. Peel off the paper pattern when all the pieces have been cut out.

Spray the back of the stencil very lightly with spray adhesive to hold it in position as you apply the paint. You can use special stencil paint or any other type that is not too runny. Use the minutest quantity of paint on your brush; it helps to have a rag or some kitchen paper handy to wipe the brush almost dry each time you refresh it with colour. Use a broad, flat-tipped brush and start painting at the edges of the stencil with a dabbing or swirling motion.

Woodgraining

There was a time when all pine was grained to make it look like a more expensive hardwood; more recently the scrubbed pine look has been very much in vogue. Now the paint effects revival has reinstated the art of graining and you can buy a selection of different graining combs from most decorating shops. The combs are designed for particular wood effects, with knots and grains of different sizes. The basic idea is to paint a base colour that imitates the colour of wood, such as a golden brown, in an oil-based paint and then to cover it with a transparent glaze, known as scumble, into which you work while it is still wet. As you pull the comb through the wet glaze the raised rubber ridges leave the grain pattern behind. The effect is remarkably realistic. Simple, 'naïve-style' woodgraining, for a more rustic look, can be done with a home made comb. Follow the step-by-step guide on page 161.

One other way of woodgraining is to paint an eggshell base coat in a warm yellow or deep red-brown (depending on the type of wood you are imitating). Tint the scumble glaze to a darker shade using oil paints or stainers and brush it once with a stiff-bristled medium-sized brush, used on its side. This will give a striped, grained effect that can be softened with a dry brush. Use a small artist's brush to add details, like

WOODGRAINING

I   Paint the base colour and leave to dry. Make a graining comb from stiff cardboard. Paint on a coat of scumble glaze, which you must work while it is still wet.

2   Use a dry, stiff-bristled brush or the graining comb to imitate the grain in the wet glaze. Work from top to bottom, wiping off excess 'blobs' on the brush or comb as you go.

3   The finishing touches can be added with a twist of cork to make knots and a fine brush loaded with a darker shade to exaggerate the grain in places.

knots and deep grain. The best results come not so much from following instructions and painted examples as from careful examination of a real piece of the wood you want to copy. Try out the effect on piece of hardboard first.

Colourwashing

Colourwashing makes a soft-looking finish that looks at ease in a period house. You can make a simple, easy-to-apply colourwash by diluting emulsion paint with two parts water and one part mixed wallpaper paste. The wallpaper paste imparts a slightly gelatinous quality to the diluted paint, which makes it far less likely to run. Apply the colourwash with a decorator's sponge or large brush and keep a dry brush handy to blend any hard edges before they dry. You can also buy colour washing kits from DIY stores and specialist paint manufacturers.

Chalky paints with varnish

This is a practical and attractive way to decorate a hallway or bathroom, as it gives protection to the walls where they are most vulnerable to being touched. It is an echo of the Victorians' use of anaglypta below the dado rail for the same reasons. Choose one of the chalky-finished Mediterranean-style paints and apply two coats to the walls. Use a ruler and spirit level to draw a chalk line at dado height, then paint the lower section of the wall with clear satin varnish. The colour will deepen a few shades and have a wipe-clean surface that could well be mistaken for a 'patina of age'. You could apply a pattern to the top half of the wall using the same type of varnish with a stencil, or create a decorative border at dado height using the same technique.

Wallpaper

There are several wallpaper companies that have been producing the same patterned papers by the same hand-blocked methods for over 150 years, so if authenticity is what you are after, and you are not on a tight budget, your quest will be an easy one. The early nineteenth-century patterns were mostly classically inspired, with swags, urns, wreaths

and stripes. The French dominated wallpaper production and the Empire style of the time was passed on to other countries through the export of their wallpapers. Machine production began in the middle of the nineteenth century at the same time as a whole new colour range was made possible, thanks to the new synthetic dyes. Long rolls of complicated patterns could now be produced at a fraction of the cost of hand-blocking. What is more, the wallpaper could be pasted directly onto a plastered wall, whereas earlier papers had been hung on canvas screens that were battened to the wall. Wallpaper was suddenly all the rage.

Pugin used the new machines and dyes to produce brilliant diamond patterns with Tudor roses and other medieval patterns. You can get a good idea of the types of pattern that were used as inspiration from Owen Jones's *Grammar of Ornament* – a big book first published in 1856 and now back in print. It is in full colour and documents the evolution of pattern as seen through the eyes of a Victorian design scholar, beginning with the earliest civilizations.

Once the Victorians had discovered wallpaper they used it everywhere – so a room might have contained four or five different patterns: one raised pattern on anaglypta below the dado rail, a border pattern above it, then an intricate or flocked pattern extending up to the frieze which, like the ceiling, might also have been papered in yet another different pattern.

William Morris and the Arts and Crafts movement adopted a different approach. They hated the machinery of mass-production and returned to hand-blocking and naturally produced pigments. Morris's company, Morris & Co., eventually went out of business in the 1940s, but Sandersons have the original Morris pattern range. A selection of his wallpapers –

LEFT *Using white, cream and pale grey on furniture as well as walls, as the Scandinavians did in the eighteenth century, brings as much reflected light as possible into a room. Here authentically period, chalky white has been combined with blue checked fabric.*

now machine-made – can be bought from them, and from time to time they re-introduce another set of original patterns.

William Morris was not the only designer to have a big influence on wallpaper design. Walter Crane, who started as a children's book illustrator, produced very popular frieze and wallpaper patterns. Christopher Dresser used all the technology and cultural influences that were coming in from all corners of the world to design an eclectic range of stylish wallpapers. C.F.A. Voysey actually rejected Morris's ideas and created a look of his own, with much lighter colours, stylized animals, birds and plants and a very distinctive style. Baillie Scott was another influential designer who had a lot in common with Voysey – their look filtered through to the mass-produced Edwardian housing, where it blended with the Arts and Crafts and Art Nouveau styles of the time.

When *Home Front* ran a feature about William Morris, they asked Jocasta Innes to come up with an inexpensive 'Morris-style room' for the programme. Jocasta decided to rejuvenate the style by using a lovely bright yellow distemper paint on the walls. This type of paint would have been used a lot by Morris himself for his wallpapers, but not in this particular colour. She added a typical Morris feature – a shelf all the way round the walls at picture-rail height, which was stained green. Besides providing an architectural feature, this was a good place to display plates and other ceramics. The walls were stencilled with a pattern taken from one of Morris's own designs and one wall was draped with a gathered piece of Morris fabric ('Strawberry Thief' – which is still available from Liberty & Co.). Plain calico curtains were stencilled with the same pattern

to tie them in with the walls and hung at the window. Jocasta furnished the room with a simple chair, a salvaged church pew and a bench with a seat cushion. More 'Morris' style was added with tapestry cushions and cast-iron candlesticks and wall sconces.

A summary of period styles as applied to wallpaper may be helpful when you are ploughing through pattern books:

- **Georgian** – original hand-blocked papers from a specialist, or silk.

- **Regency** – Regency stripes, gold damask look.
- **Victorian** – Diamond or diaper patterns in rich colours with gold, big-flocked patterns, 'busy' florals, pictorial scenes, Chinoiserie.
- **Late Victorian** – William Morris, Japanese-influenced patterns, Voysey-stylized natural forms.
- **Edwardian** – Light colours – pink, cream, blue – with patterns of flowers, ribbons, bows, fine stripes, lace, borders to match.

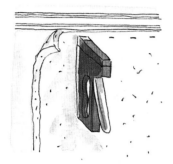 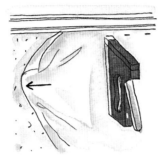 

1　Using a staple gun with long staples, cover the walls with wadding. Wooden battens along the wall will make the job easier. Measure the wall and join up lengths of fabric to fit.

2　Begin by 'tacking' the fabric up with temporary staples. Once it is hanging across the whole wall you can stretch it, levering out the first staples and putting in the permanent ones.

3　Finish off the edges of the fabric with a braid. This can be glued on and held in place with pins until bonded.

Other wall coverings

Fabric, which was used a great deal in Regency times, can easily be put up with a staple gun. If you are thinking of covering your walls this way, go to a market or factory outlet and buy a bolt (roll) of fabric. Traditionally hidden fabrics, such as mattress covering, ticking, suit lining and calico are especially cheap and can give dramatic effects, especially if you 'tent' the ceiling. To staple fabric on walls and ceilings, follow the step-by-step guide above. Muslin can also be used if it is well gathered. If your budget is tight, there are numerous ways in which you can achieve striking decorative effects with paper. Reproductions of old maps, manuscripts or music look fantastic pasted onto a wall, and are reminiscent of the black and white prints

that were pasted directly on to the walls, in paper 'frames', in the eighteenth century. Finish them off with a coat of antiquing varnish.

Brown parcel wrap can be used in place of wallpaper and looks even better after a coat of satin varnish. Print your own wallpaper on cheap lining paper using rubber or sponge stamps. This is not difficult if you have a paper pasting table. Use a piece of card as a measure between the motifs and start at the top of the roll. Use a quick-drying acrylic or emulsion paint – or try one with a chalky texture to give a slightly raised pattern.

Photocopies can be used to make effective friezes at dado or picture-rail level. Enlarge and reproduce an image of your choice on a photocopying machine (several books of authentic period motifs are now widely available); then make cut-outs if this would be more effective. Use a plumb line and pencil to mark your guidelines. Paste the photocopies along the line to make a frieze, then apply a protective coat of clear matt varnish.

LEFT *The stripped and polished natural wood fireplace surround, window shutters and floorboards, and the plain white walls make a suitable backdrop to the natural unbleached fabrics in this gently minimalist room.*

DECORATING THE WALSHES' HOUSE

When they came to choose colour schemes and decorative effects for their house, Graham and Maxine had help from a team of experts, including Jocasta Innes, Peter Plaskitt and Stewart Walton.

The hallway was decorated with Peter Plaskitt's help. The old wallpaper was stripped off and the walls cross-lined with new lining paper. The walls were then given two coats of white vinyl silk and were colourwashed in a soft creamy yellow using diluted emulsion brushed on and wiped off. They used a large Victorian-style stencil, and sprayed it on to the walls with aerosol paint (seen on page 57).

The kitchen and dining room were wallpapered with deep red and ochre/gold Designer's Guild paper, and the kitchen cupboards were given an eggshell finish in an ochre yellow that picked up the colour in the wallpaper (seen on page 132).

Stewart helped the Walshes' daughter Victoria, aged thirteen, with the colour scheme in her room. Victoria had made up a scrapbook of her favourite colours, furniture and accessories, and between them they decided to divide the walls into three sections, with the ceiling, top and bottom of the walls painted blue and the middle section given a gingham effect using small paint rollers.

Peter also helped Maxine and Graham to decorate the bathroom. The same lime green that was used on the matchboarding was used as a base coat on the upper portion of the walls. This was then stencilled with an all-over diamond pattern in blue, and another simple flower shape added within the diamonds. Graham had been sceptical about the colour scheme at the outset, but they all agreed that the end result was stunning (seen on page 147).

Jocasta tackled the 'parlour', where the newly restored fireplace took pride of place. Maxine wanted a traditional floral-patterned wallpaper and, as the Walshes already had a dusky pink sofa and chairs, they settled on a design which included that colour. The pattern was fairly overpowering until the the room was dressed with plain, but sumptuously draped calico curtains, lots of pictures and interesting pieces of furniture.

TOP RIGHT *A parlour-in-waiting – the main room as it was when the Walshes bought the house.*

RIGHT *The room had a bay window, original moulded cornices, picture-rails and fireplace, but the Walshes chose to emphasize the period feel with Victorian-style wallpaper and elaborately draped window dressing.*

finishing touches

PREVIOUS PAGES *Beachcomber's finds are displayed alongside odd pieces of china under the awning in this seaside retreat. Fabric tenting like this might be used to disguise a damaged or ugly ceiling. The shell mirror and sunhat hang from matching gingham ribbon, and all the fabrics on the chairs are casually related in pattern or colour.*

RIGHT *A light, floral theme unites furniture and objects. The chair skirt is fresh and new but sits happily alongside the antique rose-painted table.*

twelve

What are finishing touches? And where do we get them? The answer is that they are anything and can come from anywhere. So much depends upon your personality, home and lifestyle. Some people are natural collectors and hoarders, others keep throwing things away. Some like a lot of clutter and others prefer clarity and simplicity. Each to their own, but if you are restoring a period house there are things that will look and feel just right. These may be small details, like a porcelain light pull, or much larger ones, like an old solid brass fender. The right wooden towel rail, doormat or marble larder shelf can make the world of difference to an old house and these are the sort of things you should have on your mental shopping list from the word go. Never pass a skip, boot sale, flea market or reclamation yard without casting your eyes over the goods on offer, because you never know what may turn up. And never think it will still be there tomorrow, because it probably won't be.

Where to look for old things

Architectural salvage yards

If you have never visited one of these, it may be best to start with a small one, otherwise you may never emerge. Basically what happens is that demolition firms remove anything of any value from the houses, factories, shops, churches, etc, that they pull down and sell it on to reclamation or salvage yards. They sort everything out into convenient categories – outdoor stuff such as roofing tiles, pillars, stone steps, and so on; indoor stuff such as doors, windows, skirtings, archways, fireplaces, sinks, baths, etc. Then there are all the small things – taps, light switches and fittings, door furniture, stained- and etched-glass panels, knobs, brackets, decorative plasterwork and lots of

unusual individual bits and pieces that can add immediate effect to an old house.

SALVO is an organization that produces a newsletter, magazine and a directory of all the salvage yards in Great Britain, Ireland and France. If you are interested in scouring the countryside for particular items you can obtain from them a comprehensive county-by-county sheet (see page 186).

This sheet lists all architectural salvage yards within the county, as well as providing details of any specialization (bathroom fittings, for instance). SALVO also lists demolition yards, local restorers and craftspeople with particular skills. Look out for their sign when you visit a salvage yard, because it guarantees that the goods were honestly come by. They run a 'Theft Alert' page in their magazine and on their web site on the Internet. The magazine carries advertisements and articles about unusual things on offer and sought after. It is invaluable.

Car boot sales

Believe it or not, there are still people who clear out their attics and sheds and have never watched the *Antiques Road Show* or read an antiques price guide. There is also a tremendous amount of genuine rubbish. Train yourself to have a selective eye and never pass a boot sale without giving the stalls the once-over. A lot of people are there to buy their children toys and clothes and would think you mad to buy a chipped enamel bucket, but scrubbed up it may be just the thing for your Victorian kitchen. Look

LEFT *Collections make great displays, and these old glass jelly moulds and bottles are shown off to perfection by dark green walls, simple shelves and good lighting.*

RIGHT *Glimmers of gold and silver – the curtain pole over the doorway, the mirror frames and glass baubles in the fireplace – and deep claret-coloured walls transform what might have been an ordinary collection of books into a rich, eye-catching scene.*

Junk shops, flea markets and antique fairs

As with car boot sales, you develop an eye for things among the piles of clutter in junk shops. If you have any locally, it is a good idea to pop in frequently. You will soon recognize the new stock and may be lucky enough to beat antique dealers to it – they will be doing the same thing. The seaside is a happy hunting ground, for the sad reason that many elderly people retire there and eventually and inevitably leave behind their worldly goods. Flea markets are groups of small semi-organized stalls that deal at the bottom end of the antique trade. It is possible to pick up bargains, but dealers will already have made their selection. As with junk shops, regular attendance pays dividends.

Antique fairs are worth visiting because a lot of the dealers are part-timers who trade from fairs and market stalls. Not having a shop to fill, they hope to go home with an empty van and will often knock prices down rather than load everything up again at the end of the day. You will also come across specialists at fairs, who deal in just one area – it could be old enamel advertising signs, French storage jars or tapestry samplers. Antique fairs are a visual feast and are worth going to, even if you are only shopping for ideas.

Auctions

Auctions can be nerve-racking, but once you get over the initial terror and actually put in a successful bid, they seem a lot less daunting. Start by attending a small one. Go to the

out for interesting wooden items coated with gloss paint – kitchen towel rails, sets of containers, stools and boxes. People often get rid of things like this because the plastic versions are lighter and easier to keep clean. Old sets of scales are thrown out in favour of new electronic ones and wooden garden chairs rejected because they need constant repainting. All these, and more, can be yours if you look.

viewing and have a good look over everything on offer. Each item will have a lot number and be listed in the sale catalogue, with a brief description. There may be a reserve price, which means that the owner will not accept anything less, but you could get it for just one pound more. If you really want something but cannot face the idea of bidding against people on the spur of the moment, you can leave a bid with the auctioneer. If the price does not rise above the amount you offer, yours will be the successful bid. Theoretically you should get it for less if the bidding does not rise to your offered price, but consider it a bonus if you do.

If you decide to bid in the auction, bear in mind that the auctioneer probably knows most of the regular faces and is used to their little nods and winks. You will need to make your bid more obvious – and don't be afraid to scratch your nose or blink if you have to, as auctioneers always double-check with a newcomer.

If your bid is immediately upped over and over again, the chances are you are bidding against a determined dealer who can afford to pay more, so stick to a pre-set top limit, or the thrill of victory could be very expensive.

Antique shops and markets

These operate at all levels, from exorbitantly priced fine items to cheap and cheerful bric-à-brac. Never take young children eating ice cream into the best ones, but on the other hand don't be put off having a look around either. You may see a perfect object costing the earth in one shop and then find the same thing with chips and cracks going for a song down the road. Collectors have little interest in damaged goods, but you can work wonders with a tube of glue. Better to own something beautiful, old and cracked than something new, bland and perfect – especially if it is a Staffordshire jug or a lovely china charger.

Picture frames are often piled up in corners because they need repairs or new glass. They can be fixed with modelling material and painted or gilded. Make a habit of dropping in to local antique shops and tell them if there is something in particular that you are looking for; they all know each other's stock and will enjoy the satisfaction of helping you get what you want.

Reproductions

There are a lot of companies dealing in fittings and fixtures for the traditional-home market. Whether you are looking for original-style brass wall lights, a porcelain Belfast sink or cast-iron kettle for an Aga – be assured that there is someone out there who can supply it. Some things are still made by the original companies, trading for over 200 years and still using the same tools, patterns and machinery. Others are new companies, set up by people who appreciate the craftsmanship of the past and want to step back from the rat race to enjoy the quiet creativity of basket-weaving or wood-turning. There are also the chain stores who produce a sort of 'theme-park' version of Victorian and Edwardian-style goods – mass-produced in the most economically viable Far Eastern country of the moment. An old house will cringe at these lightweight fakes – it is far better to buy something contemporary that is well designed.

There is no reason why everything in an old house should be old. Some things, like electrical and plumbing fittings, need updating and the new designs are safer and more efficient than the old. You can buy brass telephone jack plugs, wall sockets and dimmer switches that comply with all the latest safety standards but look as if they have been around for a hundred years or more. Brass taps for both kitchen sinks and bathrooms are better bought new, because of new pipe sizes and types of hot-water systems. You may fall in love with the look of a set of pillar taps in a junk shop, but do check whether there is a new version of the same style on the market before you buy them, because reconditioning and adapting them could cost more than a new set. The same applies to toilet seats: old-style toilets do not have the same fixings as new ones and you could get stuck with a wonky, ill-fitting seat.

If you are looking for particular items that need to fit, it is a good idea to make a sketch, with measurements, or even to take a photograph of the type of fixtures you have. Take measurements of openings, depths and heights of any spaces that you intend to fill and carry a tape measure everywhere you go. Things like grates come in a surprisingly large selection of shapes, and waving your hands around to show the size you need just won't do.

Finishing touches to look out for

Starting at the front door, look out for a knocker, knob, letterplate and numbers made of brass or antique ironwork. Nice old bells, cast-iron boot scrapers, new doormats and flower pots in proportion to the size of the doorway will all enhance the entrance.

A large old mirror or hall stand gives character to an entrance hall, and a coat rail or two and an umbrella stand will avoid piles of clutter.

Dress up your windows with grand curtains and pelmets or wooden shutters on the inside. Second-hand curtain shops are a particularly good source for large houses with big, old bay windows and very high ceilings. Replace new

LEFT *The shape of the roof and the porthole window in this attic room are so unusual that the owner has wisely chosen not to introduce anything that would detract from them. Simple pull-up blinds and a pale, single colour scheme make the room seem lighter and more spacious.*

BELOW *This could be a very ordinary bathroom but grandeur has been added with a large antique mirror, drapes at the window and an old, silver-painted radiator. Surround a new mirror with mouldings then gild or paint them, drape muslin at the windows and fill a jug with big flowers for a similar effect.*

doors with old reclaimed ones and buy interesting door handles – there are some wonderful old and new designs. Old woven Turkish or Indian rugs may be cleaned and mended. Even fairly threadbare rugs have a 'presence' – think 'shabby chic'. New ethnic rugs and folk art styles, like pictorial rag rugs, look good on polished floorboards.

Kitchens can be filled with lovely old plates, jars, tins and bottles. An old clothes airer can be hung with implements, shelves dressed up with fabric borders, windows topped with pelmets, and framed pictures, mirrors and a blackboard hungon the wall. Hang bunches of herbs on hooks under shelves and find room for unusual corner cupboards, spice racks or salt boxes – they all add character.

Fill the bathroom with things to look at as you laze in the bath: collections of shells, buttons, soap dishes or seaside souvenirs. Bathroom and loo walls can be covered with framed postcards or black and white photographs of relatives long gone – yours or somebody else's. Make a mosaic from old

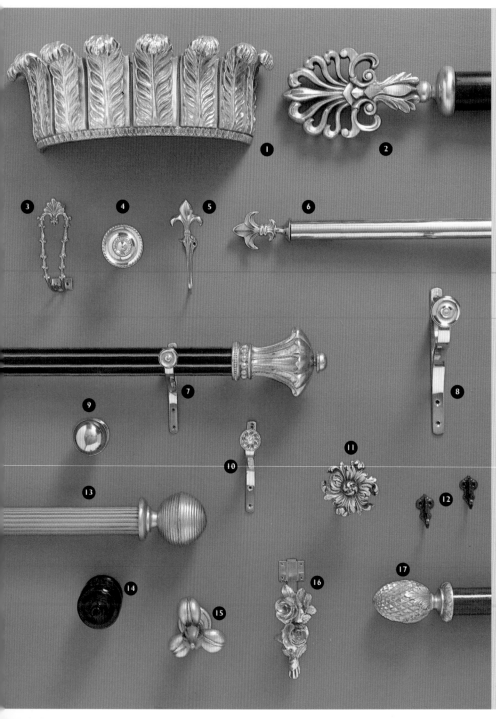

Reproduction Curtain Accessories

1 **Ostrich feather corona**
   (Georgian/Regency)
2 **Athimium finial and wooden pole**
   (Georgian/Regency)
3 **Traditional holdback**
   (Georgian/Edwardian)
4 **Holdback**
   (Gothic Revival)
5 **Fleur-de-lis holdback**
   (Gothic Revival)
6 **Fleur-de-lis finial with brass pole**
   (Gothic Revival)
7 **Empire style finial, pole and bracket**
   (Regency)
8 **Brass bracket**
   (Suits most brass poles)
9 **Ball end finial**
   (Edwardian)
10 **Rose rosette bracket**
   (Victorian)
11 **Fleur holdback**
   (Victorian)
12 **Ironwork holdbacks**
   (Arts and Crafts)
13 **Ribbed ball finial and reeded pole**
   (Regency)
14 **Gothic polished wood finial**
   (Victorian)
15 **Lotus finial**
   (Victorian)
16 **Floribunda holdback**
   (Edwardian/Victorian)
17 **Pineapple finial and wooden pole**
   (Regency)

1   Soften modelling material (available from craft shops) with your fingers then press it onto the frame to fill any gaps; knead shapes that are roughly similar in shape to missing details.

2   Use a modelling tool while the material is still soft, and then, when it is dry and hard, a metal file to make the repair match the rest of the frame. Paint, or cover with size and gild.

broken bits of china to cover an unexciting vase, or frame a mirror. Find ferns that thrive in the atmosphere. Fit wall sconces for candles and replace a utilitarian bathroom shelf with a wooden wall cupboard.

For bedrooms, look out for white woven bedcovers, lace-edged pillow slips, unusual table lamps and upholstered chairs. Have bookshelves, made from MDF but finished off with wooden mouldings and architrave to blend with the other woodwork, built into alcoves. Look out for old hooks for the back of the door and, if you have a central light, make sure the size of the lampshade is in proportion to the room. Old bed frames are not always expensive and new mattresses can be made to fit any size. Make sure any iron bed you buy has all its bits, though – they need connecting irons which come in several different types, and some are hard to find.

Children's rooms should be for them to fill, so indulge yourself while they are babies. Wooden cribs, toys and chests and old teddy bears are wonderfully nostalgic. Nursery furniture and accessories are highly collectable, too, so you could think of them as an investment for the future.

Finishing touches don't have to be old or nostalgic. Try to go to one of the big annual events, like the *Country Living* Fair in London, or any local crafts fairs that are often showcases for craftspeople with great talent, individuality and new ideas. Write to the Crafts Council (see page 186) and ask for their list of recommendations – people working in all areas of arts and crafts who will work to individual commissions. Give them a chance to make things today that will be appreciated in the future with the same enthusiasm that we now feel for the crafts of the past.

THE WALSHES' FINISHING TOUCHES

J ocasta Innes showed Maxine and Graham several tricks of the trade to add a few finishing touches to their house with minimal outlay.

Restoring a stucco frame

Having the 'right' things on the wall lends an air of authenticity to a period-style room. When Maxine and Jocasta went bargain hunting in a local junk shop, they returned with a damaged Victorian gilded picture frame which would be perfect for the parlour.

The frame was very ornate and some pieces were missing from the moulding. The first thing to do was clean it. Household vinegar was used to remove the surface grime. Using special modelling clay and a sculptor's modelling tool (bought from an artist's suppliers), Jocasta filled the gaps in the moulding and made shapes to match the rest of the frame. These were given a

final modelling with a file once the clay was dry. (See the step-by-step guide on page 183.)

The new sections were the painted gold and 'antiqued' to blend in with the old mouldings, by having a small amount of raw umber oil paint rubbed on them. (You could gild the repaired frame with real gold, following the step-by-step guide to gilding on page 92.) The repairs were quite invisible; the completed frame looked convincingly old.

Making silhouette pictures

Long before photography was invented, people used to have their silhouettes painted, and then framed and displayed. Jocasta showed Maxine and Graham how to trace their profiles off Polaroid photographs on to acetate film so that they could be photocopied and enlarged. The silhouettes were then filled in with black ink, cut out and framed. They looked like authentic antiques – only close examination revealed them to be Maxine and Graham.

Painting old furniture

Maxine had a small occasional table that she thought was worthless; she was about to throw it out when Jocasta persuaded her that it could be transformed with paint effects, especially as it had a good shape. Jocasta's idea was to paint it, and add a pattern, a flowery lyre, in gold on the top, and line the edges with a thin gold line. They chose a ready-made pattern, but you could take any image from a book, and enlarge or reduce it to the right size using tracing paper on a photocopier.

The table immediately looked much better when it had been rubbed down and given a coat of matt dark green paint. Jocasta then showed Maxine how to use chalky transfer paper (available from craft shops) to transfer the pattern of the motif to the table top,

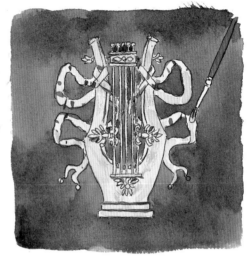

I   Secure the pattern in position over the transfer paper with a small piece of masking tape. Trace down the pattern with a sharp hard lead pencil.

2   Fill in the pattern with gold gouache paint using a fine artist's brush. Start at the outside edges to make a clean line, and then fill in the rest.

advising her to cut down the transfer paper to the same size as the motif. The motif was painted in gold gouache paint using small- and medium-sized artist's brushes. Jocasta advised Maxine to 'let the brush make the shape for you'. To achieve a similar effect, follow the step-by-step instructions above.

They completed the transformation of the table by lining the edges using a gold felt-tipped pen with a straight-edged ruler – an easy way to add a gold border to any piece of furniture.

RIGHT *The restored gilded picture frame, the painted table top and Maxine and Graham immortalized in silhouette.*

USEFUL ADDRESSES

General and Chapters 1–3

The British Institute of Architectural
Technologists (BIAT)
397 City Road
London EC1V 1NE
Tel: 0171 278 2206

The Building Centre Bookshop
26 Store Street
London WC1E 7BT
Tel: 0171 637 3151

The Conservation Unit
Museums and Galleries Commission
16 Queen Anne's Gate
London SW1H 9AA
Tel: 0171 233 3683
For a fee, information is provided on
up to five conservation workshops. A
range of leaflets is also available.

The Crafts Council
44a Pentonville Road
Islington
London N1 9BY
Tel: 0171 278 7700
Fax: 0171 837 6891

English Heritage
Fortress House
23 Savile Row
London W1X 2HE
Tel: 0171 973 3000

The Georgian Group
37 Spital Square
London E1 6DY
Tel: 0171 387 1720

Goddard and Gibbs Studios
41-49 Kingsland Road
London E2 2AJ
Tel: 0171 739 6563
Stained glass specialists

LASSCO
Mark Street
(off St Paul Street)
London EC2A 4ER
Tel: 0171 739 0448
Enormous selection of architectural
reclamation. Send S.A.E. for brochure
and current clearance list

The Lime Centre
Long Barn
Morestead
Winchester SO21 1LZ
Tel: 01962 713 636

The National Heating Consultancy
(NHC)
PO Box 370
London SE9 2RP
Tel: 0181 294 2442

The National Inspection Council for
Electrical Installation Contracting
(NICEIC)
37 Albert Embankment
London SE1 7UJ
Tel: 0171 582 7746
Fax: 0171 820 0883

The National Council of Master
Thatchers Associations
12 Green Finch Drive
Moulton
Northampton NN3 7HX
Tel: 07000 781 909

The Royal Institute of British
Architects (RIBA)
66 Portland Place
London W1N 4AD
Tel: 0171 580 5533

The Royal Institute of Chartered
Surveyors (RICS)
12 Great George Street
London SW1P 3AD
Tel: 0171 334 3842/3838/3819

SALVO
Ford Woodhouse
Berwick on Tweed
Northumberland TD15 2QF
Tel: 01668 216 494
Fax: 01668 216 494
Architectural salvage listings magazine.

The Society for the Protection of
Ancient Buildings (SPAB)
37 Spital Square
London E1 6DY
Tel: 0171 377 1644

The Victorian Society
1 Priory Gardens
London W4 1TT
Tel: 0181 994 1019

Walcot Reclamation
The Depot
Riverside Business Park
Lower Bristol Road
Bath BA2 3DW
Tel: 01225 335532
Architectural salvage. Send S.A.E. for
brochure.

Chapter 4

The Guild of Architectural
Ironmongers
8 Stepney Green
London E1 3JU
Tel: 0171 790 3431

Chapter 6

A. Bell & Co. Ltd
Kingsthorpe Road
Kingsthorpe
Northamptonshire NN2 6LT
Tel: 01604 712505
Enquiries about marble and stone
cleaning products.

Antique Fireplaces
The Manor House
Tarvin Village
Cheshire CH3 8EB
Tel: 01829 740 936

Colne Stoves & Fireplaces
Brook Hil Park
42 Halstead Road
Earlscolne
Colchester CO6 2NL
Tel: 01787 222 608
Fax: 01787 223 586

Council for Registered Gas Installers
(CORGI Gas Watchdog)
1 Elmwood
Chineham Business Park
Crockford Lane
Basingstoke
Hants RG24 8WG
Tel: 01256 37230

The Decorative Gas Fire
Manufacturers' Association
10 Freemantle Business Centre
Millbrook Road East
Southampton SO15 1JR
Tel: 01703 631593
Fax: 01703 634497

The National Association of Chimney
Sweeps (NACS)
St Mary's Chambers
19 Station Road
Stone
Staffordshire ST15 8JP
Tel: 01785 811732

The National Fireplace Association
PO Box 1200
Freepost BN2043
Birmingham B11 2BD
Freephone: 0800 52 1611

The Solid Fuel Association
Old School House
Church Street
Sutton-in-Ashfield
Nottinghamshire NG17 1AE
Tel: 0800 600 000
Fax: 01623 44 1249

Chapter 8

The British Carpet Manufacturers'
Assocation
5 Portland Place
London W1N 3AA
Tel: 0171 580 7155
Information on all types of carpeting.

Crucial Trading
The Market Hall
Craven Arms
Shropshire SY7 9NY
Tel: 01588 673 666
Natural flooring – good mail-order
service.

Fired Earth
Twyford Mill
Oxford Road
Adderbury
Oxfordshire OX17 3HP
Tel: 01295 812088
Tiles, stone and natural matting
carpets.

Forbo-Nairn
PO Box 1
Kirkcaldy
Fife KY1 2SB
Tel: 01592 643 111
Sheet lino and borders.

HSS Hire Shops
Tel: 0800 282 8282
Floor sanders and other hire
equipment – phone for local branch
addresses and phone numbers.

J. Price Stair Rods
118 Guernsey Road
Liverpool L13 6RY
Tel: 0115 947 5430
Traditional and their own original-style
stair rods. Mail order.

Original Style
Stovax Limited
Falcon Road
Sowton Industrial Estate
Exeter
Devon EX2 7LF
Tel: 01392 474 058
Victorian encaustic tiled floors –
reproductions from original moulds.

Wicanders
Amorium House
Star Road
Partridge Green
Horsham
West Sussex RH13 8RA
Tel: 01403 710002
Corktiles – coloured and natural, also
woodstrip, floors.

Chapter 9

Andrew Macintosh Ltd
Unit 1–2
Grenfell Place
Maidenhead
Berkshire SL6 1HL
Tel: 01628 73550
Shaker and bespoke kitchens

Antique Fireplaces
The Manor House
Tarvin Village
Cheshire CH3 8ED
Tel: 01829 740936
Traditional kitchen ranges

Brass & Traditional Sinks Ltd
Devauden Green
Near Chepstow
Gwent NP6 6PL
Tel: 01291 650738
Reproduction taps and butler's sinks

Country Cookers
Bruff Works
Bushbank
Suckley
Worcestershire WR6 5DR
Tel: 01886 884262
Reconditioned Agas.

The Yorkshire Range Company
Church Lane
Halston East
Skipton
North Yorkshire BD23 6EH
Tel: 01756 710263
Nationwide service for traditional
kitchen ranges.

Chapter 10

The British Bathroom Council
Federation House
Stoke-on-Trent
Staffordshire ST4 2RT
Tel: 01782 747 074
Fax: 01782 747 161

Chapter 11
TRADITIONAL PAINTS

Brats
281 Kings Road
London SW3 5EW
Tel: 0171 351 7674
Mediterranean colours – a range of
water-based chalky-finish paints.
Colours from vivid to soft – good
range.

Craig & Rose
172 Leith Walk
Edinburgh EH6 5EB
Tel: 0131 554 1131
Floorpaints, masonry nails, lead paints
(only for Grade I & II listed buildings),
tile primer.

Farrow & Ball
33 Uddens Trading Estate
Wimborne
Dorset BH21 7NL
Tel: 0202 876 141
National Trust range of paints in
historic colours – estate emulsion,
distempers, gloss, dead-flat oil and oil
undercoat. Sample pots on sale in
National Trust shops.

Fired Earth
Twyford Mill
Oxford Road
Adderbury
Oxfordshire OX17 3HP
Tel: 01295 812088
In conjunction with the Victoria &
Albert Museum. Small authentic range
of historic colours in emulsion,
eggshell, dead-flat oil and distemper.

Heritage Village Paints
Swinfen
Nr Lichfield
Staffordshire WS14 9QR
Tel: 01543 481 612
Milk paints and acrylic latex in
traditional colours imported from
USA. Also available from the Shaker
Shop (Tel: 0171 724 7672) – ask for
suppliers' list with colour charts.

Paint Magic (mail-order dept)
79 Shepperton Road
London N1 3DF
Tel: 0171 354 9696
Paint-effect kits, traditional colours,
distempers, glazes, stencils, brushes,
colour wash, etc.

Potmolen Paints
27 Woodcock Industrial Estate
Warminster
Wiltshire BA12 9DX
Tel: 01985 213 960
Historic colours, finishes for interior
and exterior, including limewash,
distemper, colour wash, lime putty and
many more conservation and natural
products.

Rose of Jericho
Westhill Barn
Evershot
Dorchester
Dorset DT2 0LD
Tel: 01935 83662
Manufacturers of traditional paints –
limewash and distempers in a lovely
range of soft colours. Natural
pigments.

WALLPAPERS

Arthur Sanderson & Sons Ltd
52 Berners Street
London W1P 3AD
Tel: 0171 635 7800
William Morris range, plus all the rest!

Cole & Son
142 Offord Road
London N1 1NS
Tel: 0171 607 4288
Factory featured on *Home Front*.
Hand-blocked authentic historic
papers and other machine-made
versions.

Colefax & Fowler
39 Brook Street
London W1Y 2JE
Tel: 0171 493 2231
Eighteenth- and nineteenth-century
designs. Chintz patterns, *trompe-l'oile*,
borders, braids.

Laura Ashley
150 Bath Road
Maidenhead
Berks SL6 4YS
Tel: 01628 39151
Traditional style at affordable prices.

Osborne & Little
304 Kings Road
London SW3 5UH
Tel: 0171 352 1456
Eighteenth- and nineteenth-century
patterns plus their own
contemporary range.

Warner & Sons
7–11 Noel Street
London W1V 4AL
Tel: 0171 439 2411
Reproduction period wallpapers from
1800 onwards plus fabrics.

Zoffany Ltd
63 South Audley Street
London W1Y 5BF
Tel: 0171 824 8265
Hand-printed collection plus others
ranging from mid-eighteenth century
to Art Deco patterns.

Chapter 12

For SALVO and general architectural
salvage companies, *see under* **General
and Chapters 1–3**

Beardmore & Co
3–4 Percy Street
London W1P 0EJ
Tel: 0171 637 7041
Fax: 0171 436 9222
Architectural ironmongers since 1860.

Byron & Byron
4 Manor Yard
off Noel Road
London N1 8BE
Tel: 0171 704 9290
Many styles of ornamental
curtain poles.

Christopher Wray's Lighting
Emporium
591 Kings Road
London SW6 2YW
Tel: 0171 736 8434
Antique and reproduction lighting.
Send for illustrated catalogue.

Country Antique Fairs
PO Box 15
Burnham-on-Sea
Somerset TA 8 2JU
Tel: 01278 784 912
Details of big events.

IACF
PO Box 100
Newark
Nottinghamshire NG24 1DJ
Tel: 01636 702 326
Details of big antique fairs.

Olivers Lighting Company
6 The Broadway
Crockenhill
Swanley
Kent BR8 8JH
Tel: 01322 614 224
Authentically styled brass light
switches and electrical accessories.

The Curtain Exchange
Branches in: London, Essex,
Gloucestershire, Wiltshire, Cheshire,
Sussex, Buckinghamshire,
Nottinghamshire, Glasgow, Somerset,
Suffolk, Yorkshire and North Wales
Tel: 0171 731 8316 for details.
Second-hand, top-quality curtain
exchange.

BIBLIOGRAPHY

Barrett, Helen and Phillips, John, *Suburban Style*, Mitchell Beazley, 1994

Beard, Geoffrey, *Decorative Plasterwork in Great Britain*, Phaidon, 1975

Cork, Alison, *The Streetwise Guide to Renovating Your House*, Piatkus, 1995

Cunnington, Pamela, *Care for Old Houses*, A & C Black, 1991

Durrant, Stuart, *Victorian Ornamental Design*, Academy Editions, 1972

Fry, Eric C. *Buying a House?* David & Charles, 1983

Gilliat, Mary *Period Decorating* Conran Octopus, 1990

Greysmith, Brenda, *Tracing the History of Your House*, Hodder & Stoughton, 1994

Nicholas Hills, *The English Fireplace*, Quiller Press, 1983

Iredale, David and Barrett, John, *Discovering Your Old House*, Shire Publications Ltd, 1994

Jackson, Albert, and Day, David, *Collins Complete Home Restoration Manual*, Collins, 1992

Johnson, Alan *How to Restore and Improve your Victorian House,* David & Charles, 1984

Miller, Judith and Martin, *Period Style*, Mitchell Beazley, 1989

Miller, Judith and Martin, *Period Details*, Mitchell Beazley, 1987

Kevin McCloud's Lighting Book, Ebury Press, 1995

Lander, Hugh, *The House Restorer's Guide*, David & Charles, 1986, 1988, 1989

Quiney, Anthony, *Period Houses*, George Philip, 1989

Saunders, Matthew, *The Historic Home Owners' Companion*, Batsford, 1987

Sloan, Annie and Gwynn, Kate, *Colour in Decoration*, Frances Lincoln, 1990

Which? Getting Work Done on Your House, WHICH BOOKS Consumers' Association, 1988

Which Way to Clean It, WHICH BOOKS Consumers' Association, 1994

Period Living & Traditional Homes Magazine, EMAP ELAN

PICTURE CREDITS

BBC Books would like to thank the following for providing photographs and for permission to reproduce copyright material. While every effort has been made to trace and acknowledge all copyright holders, we would like to apologise should there have been any errors or omissions.

Page 2-3 Lu Jeffery; 5 Arcaid; 7 © BBC; 9 Elizabeth Whiting Assocs; 10-11 Elizabeth Whiting Assocs; 13 Pictures For Print; 14, 14-15 Edifice; 15 Pictures For Print; 18 Paul Bricknell © BBC; 19 © BBC ; 20-21 Elizabeth Whiting Assocs; 23 Welbeck Golin/Harris; 24 Elizabeth Whiting Assocs; 26, 31 Abode; 35 Lucinda Lambton/Arcaid; 37 T © BBC, Main Lucinda Symons; 38-39 Edifice; 40 Edifice; 42 Simon Rae Scott/ Architectural Association; 47 Elizabeth Whiting Assocs; 51 Justin Paul/Arcaid; 57 inset © BBC, 57 main Lucinda Symons, 60 Elizabeth Whiting Assocs; 61, 63 Houses & Interiors; 64 Rentokil; 65 Robert Harding Picture Library; 66-67 Elizabeth Whiting Assocs; 69 Robert Harding Picture Library; 73 Elizabeth Whiting Assocs; 81 Elizabeth Whiting Assocs; 82-83 Houses & Interiors; 85 Elizabeth Whiting Assocs; 86 Abode; 88-89 Abode; 93 T © BBC, B Paul Bricknell © BBC; 94-95 Abode; 97 Robert Harding Picture Library; 100-101 Elizabeth Whiting Assocs; 104 Houses & Interiors; 105 James Mortimer/The Interior Archive; 106-107 *Period Living and Traditional Homes*/Rowland Roques O'Neil; 108 Abode; 113 Phil Braham; 114-115 Wayne Vincent/The Interior Archive; 117 Simon Brown/The Interior Archive;118-119 Elizabeth Whiting Assocs; 120-121 Abode; 123 Elizabeth Whiting Assocs; 124 Robert Harding Picture Library; 127 Abode; 132 Lucinda Symons; 133 T © BBC, B Lucinda Symons; 134-135 Abode; 137 Robert Harding Picture Library; 140-141 Lu Jeffery; 143 Simon Brown/The Interior Archive; 144-145 Elizabeth Whiting Assocs; 147 T © BBC; 147 B Lucinda Symons; 148-149 Elizabeth Whiting Assocs; 152-153 Simon Brown/The Interior Archive; 156-157 Abode; 160-161 Abode; 162 Abode; 164-165 *Period Living and Traditional Homes*/Spike Powell; 166 Abode; 169 T © BBC; 169 B Lucinda Symons;170-171 Robert Harding Picture Library; 173, 174 Robert Harding Picture Library; 175 Henry Wilson/The Interior Archive; 176-177 Robert Harding Picture Library; 179 Abode; 180, 181 Lu Jeffery; 185 Lucinda Symons.

All still life photography by Paul Bricknell © BBC. BBC Books are grateful to those who kindly loaned the objects that appear on the following pages:

page 48: 1, 3, 6, 7, 9, 10, 12, 17, J.D. Beardmore; 2, 4, 15, A Touch of Brass; 5, 8, 11, 13, 14, 16, Baileys
page 70: 4, 9, Bailey's; 2, 5, 6, 11, 12, 13, 14, 15, 16, 19, J.D. Beardmore;1, 3, 7, 8, 10, 17, 18, A Touch of Brass
pages 76 & 77: 2, 3, 7, 10, 12, 14, Stevensons of Norwich;1, 9, Locker & Riley; 4, 5, 6, 8, 11, 13, 15, 16, 17, 18, Hayles & Howe
page102: 3, 5, 7, 8, 10, Richard Burbridge;1, 4, 6, Meer End;2, 9, The Cast Iron Shop
page138: 9, 17, The Top Stock Company;18, Swadling Brassware; 1, 2, 3, 4, 5, 6, 7, 8, 10, 12, 14, 15, 16, 19, 20, The Water Monopoly;11, 13, Bailey's
page151: 14, 15, Heritage Colours by Dulux;1, 8, 9, Warner Fabrics; 2, 6, Ramm, Son & Crocker; 3, 7, Cole & Son; 4 + 5, Zoffany; 10, Osborne & Little; 11, Sandersons; 12, 13, Farrow & Ball
page154: 1, 7, 8, Sanderson; 2, Ramm, Son & Crocker; 3, 10, Osborne & Little; 4, 5, Warner Fabrics; 6, Liberty 9, Anna French; 11, 12, Farrow & Ball; 13, 14, Heritage Colours by Dulux
page158: 9, Ramm, Son & Crocker; 10, 13, Definitions by Dulux; 11, 12, Heritage Colours by Dulux; 1, 3, Osborne & Little; 2, Sanderson; 4, 5, Cole & Son'; 6, 7, Warner Fabrics
page182: 1, 2, 8, 11, 15, 16, 17, Tempus Stet; 3, 4, Harrison Drape; 5, 6, 7, 9, 10, 13, 14, Cope & Timmins; 12, J.D. Beardmore

INDEX

Page numbers in *italics* refer to illustrations and captions

THE HOME FRONT GUIDE